JUNK
genius

JUNK
genius

Stylish ways to repurpose
everyday objects, with
over 80 projects and ideas

Juliette Goggin and Stacy Sirk

photography by Holly Jolliffe

CICO BOOKS
LONDON NEW YORK

From Juliette:
To Robin, I simply couldn't have done all this without your help and encouragement.

From Stacy:
To Vicke, for all the fun we have finding our treasures, and to Martin and Ryan, who never complain about tripping over them.

Published in 2012 by CICO Books
An imprint of Ryland Peters & Small Ltd
20–21 Jockey's Fields   519 Broadway
London   5th Floor
WC1R 4BW   New York
                               NY 10012

www.cicobooks.com

10 9 8 7 6 5 4 3 2 1

Text © Juliette Goggin and Stacy Sirk 2012
Design and photography © CICO Books 2012

A CIP catalog record for this book is available from the Library of Congress and the British Library.

ISBN: 978 1 908170 83 5

Printed in China

Project editor: Dawn Bates
Editor: Helen Ridge
Designer: Laura Woussen
Photographer: Holly Jolliffe
Styling: Stacy Sirk and Juliette Goggin

For digital editions, visit
www.cicobooks.com/apps.php

Contents

Introduction

Both of us had been approached separately about writing a book but although we loved the idea, there never seemed to be enough time to do it. It could easily have stayed as just a great project for one day in the future. But last year, the time seemed right, the opportunity was there, and we decided to join forces, thinking that sharing the work would really make it possible, and we were right!

We knew each other initially through work and realized that we had a common love of making and repurposing things for ourselves and for our day jobs. It's been a joyous process to collaborate. In spite of living and working in two different countries and balancing challenging schedules, we have kept to our writing and our photoshoot schedules, despite shocking weather!

Wherever you live, you can locate your equivalent of thrift stores (charity shops), junk stores, flea markets, and car boot sales and find the most amazing resources to inspire all kinds of creations. So much of the thrill is about not knowing what you might discover on any given day. Shopping is about finding known things; junking is about unearthing the unexpected in unlikely places. Somehow this random slow seeking-out is very therapeutic! Every time you use or wear something you have made from a unique find, you will savor the memory of its discovery, which gives your creation a unique and special quality.

You can also feel good about saving money, being thrifty, and rescuing something from landfill, as well as being a part of the exciting international community of crafters. Just the fun of being creative and making something that truly is one-of-a-kind is hugely enjoyable.

Repurposing the old and the odd needs a practised eye, which you will quickly gain, if you are not already a seasoned junker. Don't think our projects used up a lifetime supply of foraged items—they didn't, and we are confident you can find most of the things on our list of 40 Common Items on just a few outings. And if you spread the word about what you are looking for, raw materials for repurposing will arrive at your door. It really is that easy.

Filling your home with well-made, useful, and beautiful things that had a previous life will enrich it and make it more individual. These hand-crafted pieces will regularly attract the most enthusiastic compliments, to which you can happily reply, "I made it myself!" This way of life becomes distinctly addictive as your crafting projects become the envy of those around you. Our own experience has also taught us that a creative passion can be passed on to some of the most unlikely people, once they find the inspiration to begin.

When we first started to write this book, we had four main aims. We wanted to pass on our accumulated knowledge and love of crafting, as well as inspiring readers to try something different, find new kinds of treasures and possibilities, and develop or rediscover a love of making things. We hope we have achieved all four.

Finding Junk

Flea markets, car boot sales, junk shops, thrift stores (charity shops), garage sales, estate sales, collectors' fairs, and even the odd swishing event (a fashion swap of clothing and accessories) are great opportunities for finding real gems to turn into something new and special.

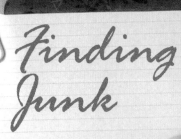

Checking with friends and family can also produce an enormous amount of things, and often items they have no idea they have. Be sure to share the love—giving them one of your creations made from their cast-offs is so rewarding and enormous fun!

An often overlooked resource is what you have squirreled away over time. It's amazing what sorting through a cupboard or two can produce, and what a happy and satisfying chore it is. Clean out your jewelry box, sort through coins from vacations abroad, have a purge of your wardrobe... All these efforts produce not only order and bags of things to dispose of but also some great candidates for a number of repurposing projects. There is something very pleasing about handling the pieces you choose to keep, washing them and setting them aside ready and gleaming for working with at a later date.

FRONT DESK

Look for items put out on the street with your neighbors' garbage (rubbish). You would be surprised at how many objects we have collected that have been "gifted" to the street.

Develop an eye for spotting treasures. If you have some projects you really want to make, keep a list of what you will need for them with you. Take your time when looking, and digging(!) through piles of what might appear to be unpromising junk. Some of the very best finds are made this way.

What's great in this feast-and-famine world of junk is that very often you won't see something for ages, then suddenly you will come across a boxful. For example, if you know that at some point you will make dessert glass candles and you unearth a collection of wonderful mixed cut or edged glasses,

buy them. Whether for gift-giving or entertaining, it's sensible to make a good quantity of the same kinds of things at once, such as poured candles, since you will probably have a good quantity of wax and wicks to use. Don't forget to have a few eggcups or tiny pans on hand if you can, to use up the extra wax.

When it comes to junk, even when it is being sold at bargain prices, be discerning. Hold out for what truly speaks to you. There will always be another opportunity, and another great find. Just when you tell yourself you will "never see one like that again," you always do!

Finding the right pieces of junk can take time but there is real fun to be had in the hunt, knowing that everything has its provenance.

40 Common Items

Wherever you live, you don't have to visit too many junk shops and flea markets to notice familiar objects turning up time and time again. The following is a selection of some of our favorite Common Items. It should only take you just a bit of searching to gather most of these junk treasures, and none of them should be expensive. Once you have found them, you will have the key to many of the projects that feature in our book. You can also use your own imagination to dream up even more ideas.

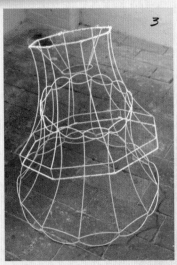

1 Old Photographs
Black-and-white, color, polaroids

2 Wallpaper
Old and new rolls, sample books

3 Lampshade Frames
Metal and white plastic-coated, with or without their shades

4 Vintage Household Linens
Sheets, pillowcases, tablecloths, napkins

5 Tape Measures
Fabric, plastic-coated, woven

6 Typewriter Keys
From old typewriters and computer keyboards, metal and plastic

7 Old Keys
Skeleton, car, luggage, clock keys, rusty or shiny

8 Wooden Measures
Yardsticks, rulers, colored and plain

9 Neckties
Silk, wool, polyester, school ties

10 Tins and Cans
Decorative vintage tins, printed food cans

11 Necklaces and Chains
Broken chains, plumber's chains, old necklaces

12 Thread Spools (Cotton Reels)
Old wooden spools, with paper end labels

13 China
Old china and porcelain oddments, tureens with or without lids

14 Glass Jars
Any type, plain or decorative

15 Souvenirs
Silk scarves, souvenir spoons, postcards, charms, all relating to a place of interest or travel

16 Old Sweaters
Great patterns such as Aran and Fair Isle, children's, hand knits

17 Glass Decanters
Cut crystal, molded, decorative

18 Lace Doilies
Crocheted, fabric insets, any size and color

19 Dishtowels (Tea Towels)
Cotton, linen, printed, and embroidered

20 Chandelier Crystals
Clear, colored, any size or shape, with or without hangers

13

12

11

14

15

16

17

18

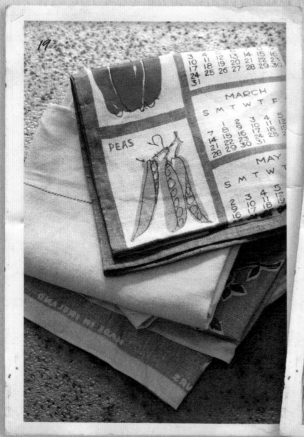

19

21 Colanders
Metal or enamel, any size

22 Drinking Glasses
Clear, straight-sided, short and tall, conical

23 Metal Items
Old silver candlesticks, scaffolding ends, closet rod ends

24 Coins
Old foreign and out-of-circulation coins

25 Picture Frames
Old wooden frames, gesso-painted, any size

26 Wire Salad Shakers
Any type with a central hole in the base

27 Tin Pans and Trays
Any type as long as they are magnetic

28 Lace and Trims
Assorted lengths of lace and trims, cotton and polyester

29 Old Paintings
Oils, watercolors, on canvas and paper

30 Denim Jackets
Old or new, to trim

31 Ceramic Shards
Broken pieces of china and porcelain

32 Folding Tables
Wooden and metal card tables

33 Buttons
Old buttons, any kind at all, with or without shanks

34 Needlepoint and Embroidery
Old needlepoints, embroideries, tapestries, hand-worked fabrics

35 Dice and Games Counters
Scrabble letters, Monopoly counters, wooden and plastic dice

36 Old Chairs
Wooden chairs, stools, small piano benches, with drop-in or wrap-around seats

37 Paper
Old giftwrap, sheet music, maps, book pages

38 Sewing Sundries
Ribbons, trims, seam binding, sewing tapes

39 Handkerchieves
Old cotton, silk, embroidered, printed, monogrammed

40 Assorted Ephemera
Paper goods such as rosettes, old letters, and receipts

36

37

38

39

40

Chapter One

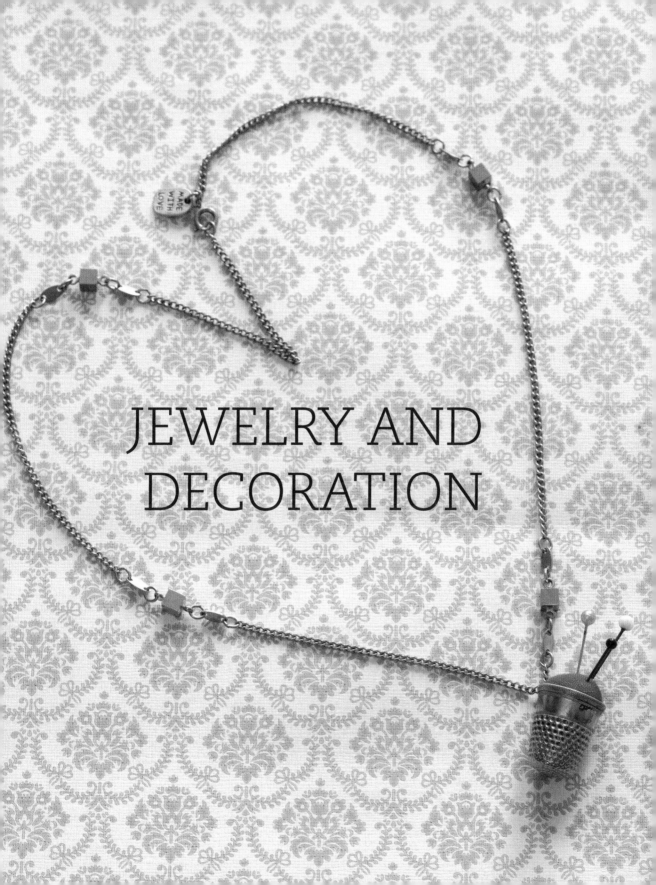

JEWELRY AND DECORATION

simple BUTTON BRACELET

This bracelet, which makes excellent use of those odd buttons that we all seem to have hanging around, can be made in as little as five minutes, provided you have all the materials to hand. It is also very simple, which means that it's a great project for children. Using an assortment of buttons makes the bracelet more interesting and unique.

Cut a length of round elastic about 4 in (10 cm) longer than the circumference of your wrist. Thread the buttons onto the elastic through the loops—they will shuffle up as you thread them and nestle together— and keep checking that the number used is sufficient to go around your wrist. When you are happy with the amount, simply tie the elastic in a knot to secure, and trim off the excess. The knot will be hidden under the buttons when the bracelet is worn.

See if you can find a few gold or silver military or
sporting-style buttons to make your bracelet extra
special. Maybe someone you know has a collection of
buttons in an old tin that they will let you use.

step-by-step BUTTON BROOCHES

These brooches are a wonderful project for showing off any beautiful spare buttons that you can't bear to throw away. Simply stack three or four buttons in graduated sizes and complementary shapes and colors, then glue them together.

☞ MATERIALS:

3–4 buttons in graduated sizes per brooch

Card or paper, as a protective surface to work on

Epoxy glue

Brooch back or old clutch pin, smaller than the largest button

1 Experiment with different buttons in colors you like until you have three or four that "nest" well together. Pile the buttons one on top of the other on card or paper, making sure that no button is completely obscured by the one on top of it.

2 Once you are happy with the arrangement, separate the buttons, put a dab of glue in the center of the largest button, and place the second button on top.

3 Repeat until you have added the last button. Move the tier of buttons to a clean piece of card or paper to dry. If glue leaks through the buttonholes, wipe off any excess with a cloth, although this shouldn't be an issue if you use the glue evenly and sparingly.

4 When the glue has dried completely and the buttons are stuck firmly together, turn them over. Apply glue to the center of the top of the bottom button and press the brooch back or clutch pin into position. Use the glue sparingly—too much and your brooch back will be sealed closed! If you're using a clutch pin, remove the clutch back before placing the pin on the glue. Wait until the glue is completely dry before reattaching it.

Instead of gluing the buttons, you can sew them together with a needle and thread. The top button can have a shank or holes, but the rest need to have the same number of holes.

simple BUTTON RING

Lift your spirits with a bit of bling! A single button can become a very flash ring. This project is really cheap and simple to make but the end result is actually quite impressive. Choose a faceted button with lots of detail. Gold and silver work particularly well.

Mix some epoxy glue well on a plate and apply it to the back of your button with a spatula. Attach it to the front of a ring blank (available from craft stores). Let the glue dry completely before wearing the ring.

simple JIGSAW PUZZLE BROOCHES

These delightful shapes come from a jigsaw puzzle aimed at very young children, so the illustrations are bright, colorful, and bold. With a brooch back, available from craft stores, glued onto the reverse, they become charming retro brooches.

Sometimes we come across odd loose jigsaw puzzle pieces, but more often we find a complete puzzle still in its original box with just a couple of pieces missing. The motifs on the vintage wooden ones are so wonderful and iconic that you just have to create something with them. As well as making brooches, you can also use them for magnets!

First of all, give your chosen puzzle piece a very gentle clean on the front, then flip it over. Mix up some epoxy glue on an old plate, ensuring that both elements are well mixed. Spread the glue thinly on the back of the piece with a toothpick or spatula and place a brooch back on top. Allow to dry, making sure the glue is fully set before pinning the brooch to your lapel.

Old wooden puzzle pieces are so charming that we always buy them when we see them, probably making up for all the ones we lost as children!

simple
SALT SPOON JEWELRY

Tiny silver or silver-plate salt and pepper spoons are beautiful objects but they are rarely used these days for their intended purpose. Instead of letting them languish away in a drawer, why not convert them into original pieces of jewelry?

Clean your salt or pepper spoons with silver polish and a soft cloth, drying them off well. Place the spoons face down onto a piece of old card or some newspaper, to protect your work surface.

For each spoon, position an old button of a similar thickness to that of the spoon about halfway underneath the end of each handle—this will allow the jump ring to dry into place at the right angle. Mix up some epoxy glue and dab a little on the tip of the handle.

Place a jump ring—this can be silver or tarnished, whichever you prefer—on the glue, with half of the ring resting on the button. When the glue is dry, fix a second jump ring to the first, then hang the spoon from the hanging loops on a kilt pin, found at craft and bead stores. Jump rings are easy to find online or at craft stores. The smaller ones are easier to handle with needlenose pliers.

These instructions can easily be adapted to make other pieces of jewelry. You can hang a single spoon from a chain to make a pendant, or glue a brooch back to the back of a spoon to create a pin.

step-by-step CERAMIC THIMBLE PENDANTS

Ceramic thimbles used to be incredibly popular as vacation souvenirs and are therefore to be found at almost every flea market and thrift store (charity shop). They are plentiful and cheap, and also make wonderful pendants hung on the simplest ironmonger's chain, thin ribbon, leather lace, or silver chain.

☞ **MATERIALS:**

Ceramic thimble

Reusable adhesive, such as Elmer's Tac (Blu Tack)

Electric drill with a very thin drill bit

Wire (24-gauge beading wire works well)

Wire cutters

Toothpick

Needlenose pliers

Chain or ribbon

Instead of wire, you can use an eye pin (a wire with a ready-made loop at one end) to make the loop for the chain. Simply thread the eye pin through the hole in the thimble with the existing eye loop inside. Then form the loop as described above, and wind the end of the eye pin under the hanging loop to form a coiled collar.

1 Secure the thimble to your work surface with reusable adhesive. This will stop it moving as you use the electric drill to make a very small hole in the top of the thimble.

2 Cut a length of wire, approximately 2½ in (6 cm) long, with wire cutters, then fold it in half. Thread the ends of the wire through the hole from underneath the thimble so the loop is inside. Using a toothpick, fold over one of the two lengths to make a loop on top of the thimble. Push the end of the wire back inside the hole in the thimble.

3 Wrap the second length of wire around the end of the loop to secure it. You may be able to do this with your fingers, otherwise use the pliers. This will form a coiled neck around the base of the loop above the top of the thimble. If necessary, adjust the loop inside the thimble so it allows the loop outside to remain upright.

4 Thread the chain or ribbon through the loop to hang the pendant.

Bead stores are a great source of all kinds of useful items, from jewelry wire to findings, many of which are used in our projects.

step-by-step
TIN PENDANTS

Although practical as pillboxes and mini sewing kits, these tiny hinged tins are so decorative that we turned them into gorgeous lockets—perfect for concealing a photo of a loved one!

☞ **MATERIALS:**

Tiny tin with a hinged or press-on lid

Small hole punch, bradawl, or electric drill with smallest drill bit

2 eye pins

Epoxy glue

Old plate

Toothpick or spatula

Needlenose pliers

Jump ring

Old chain, ribbon, or leather for necklace

1 Place the tin flat on a table. Work out the center point of the top side of the tin, and make a very small hole with the hole punch at the center point in the base of the tin, not the lid.

2 To create the hanger, twist the two eye pins together just below their eyes. Insert the pins through the hole from the outside, then spread the pins out in opposite directions around the inside edge of the tin.

3 Mix the epoxy glue well on an old plate and, with the toothpick, use it to secure the pins to the tin. Your pliers will help you bend the pins into the right shape.

4 Attach a jump ring to the loop of the eye pins with the pliers, then add your necklace chain.

simple VINTAGE BADGES

There are so many things that you can use to make original and distinctive vintage badges—these are just a few ideas to get you started.

CERAMIC BADGE

Instead of throwing away cracked and smashed cups, plates, and saucers, try using them in new ways. Look for pretty decorations such as flowers or geometric borders, or a pottery maker's name, as we have done here. Tap around the edges of the part you want to save using a small hammer—make sure you wear protective gloves and goggles, as flying china can be very sharp and dangerous!

Once you have a shape that you are reasonably happy with, smooth the rough edges by rubbing with sandpaper. Apply epoxy glue to the reverse of the ceramic and attach a brooch back. For extra bling, paint the edge with metallic gold or silver paint. If you have taken your ceramic decoration from a plate, you will have enough china left over to make plant markers (see pages 108–10).

SCRABBLE LETTER BADGE

Vintage wooden board game counters are easy to find at flea markets, either with their original games or in the bottom of a rummage box, jumbled up to give you lots of fun sorting through them! Keep a look out for letters or symbols that might have a special meaning for you or your friends and family, then turn them into truly personalized gifts. Simply apply epoxy glue to the reverse of the letter and add a clutch pin or brooch back.

MINT BOX BADGE

Small items of vintage packaging are so nostalgic and beautiful. It can be difficult to find them in perfect condition, so when you do, snap them up quickly and keep them for all sorts of gift-giving, perhaps as a container for earrings or a necklace, even chocolates or homemade candy. If the box is really small, like ours, convert it to a brooch, gluing on a brooch back with epoxy glue. You could even hide a secret message inside the box!

step-by-step
MONOPOLY COUNTER CHARM BRACELET

Old games of Monopoly are great flea-market finds, as there are so many things you can create with the contents. But the best element by far is the iconic counters, which everyone remembers. Indeed, who could forget fighting over the racing car and ending up with the old boot instead? One delightful way of reusing them is to gather them all up on a chain and wear them as a charm bracelet.

☞ **MATERIALS:**
Catch fastening and jump ring

Length of chain with wide loops, to fit your wrist,

2 wooden dice

Craft knife

2 screw eyes

Jump rings or split rings

Set of Monopoly counters

Electric drill, with a very thin drill bit

Needlenose pliers

1 Attach the catch fastening to one end of the chain and a jump ring to the other.

2 Make a small hole in each dice with the pointed end of the craft knife, then screw a screw eye into each hole. Attach a jump ring to both screw eyes, then fix the dice to the chain, one at the catch end of the chain, the other halfway along.

3 Attach jump rings to those counters that already have a hole. For those that don't, drill a small hole near the edge of the counter. Attach a jump ring through the hole and then through the chain. Space the counters evenly along the bracelet.

4 If you have a charm bracelet you no longer wear, replace the charms with Monopoly counters.

inspiration
CHARM BRACELETS

By not being made from the obvious, these charm bracelets are all the more striking and endearing. Pieces of an old necklace, metal bottle tops, medals, watch parts, brightly colored toy cars can all be turned into fantastic charm bracelets. You may even be lucky enough to find a collection of dollhouse tools, as we did, which was perfect for the job. If you decide to have silver thimbles as your charms, see the Ceramic Thimble Pendants on pages 26–7 and follow the instructions there for making hanging loops.

simple TYPEWRITER KEYS JEWELRY

Typewriter keys are fantastically stylish and make superb brooches and hat or lapel pins. You can also have a great deal of fun making up words using the letters and symbols and waiting for other people to notice them.

Mix some epoxy glue thoroughly on an old plate, then use a toothpick or spatula to apply it evenly to the backs of the typewriter keys you have chosen. Stick them onto brooch backs in groups of two or three keys, onto kilt pins (with or without loops), or hatpins. For kilt pins and hatpins, you will need to ensure the keys are supported while the glue dries so that they do not fall off.

Plastic letters and symbols from old computer keyboards can also be fun—even those from just five years ago look retro! Prise off the keys with a screwdriver, pliers, and a soft cloth to cushion the process.

KILT PIN BROOCHES

There are two types of kilt pin you can use for these brooches: the traditional kind and the decorative, found in craft and bead stores. The former has only a loop at one end, through which you can attach a jump ring or a split ring to secure a charm or other decoration.

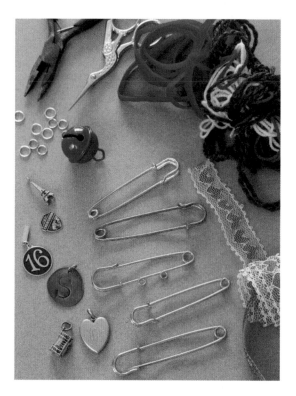

The latter has between two and four loops on one side. You can attach a number of charms to these, again using a jump ring or split ring. The advantage of this kind of pin is that the charms will remain evenly spaced and not move around when the brooch is being worn.

You could also wrap yarn (wool) or thin ribbon around the length of the pin or tie on decorations with a big colorful bow.

With a split ring you can attach a decoration with your hands, but a jump ring needs to be carefully secured with pliers so that the two ends touch and the decoration can't be pulled off accidentally.

inspiration
JEWELRY SPIN-OFFS

DOLLHOUSE JEWELRY

Even if you don't have a dollhouse, keep an eye out for all the exquisite tiny bits and pieces that are an intrinsic part of them. Dab on some epoxy glue and attach a brooch back or a jump ring and you can have yourself some really unique jewelry!

Miniature plates become arty brooches, as do overmantel mirrors and picture frames, with the addition of a vintage photograph. Tea sets and pots and pans can be added to kilt pins, while tiny tools such as hammers and spanners make fantastic earrings. Diminutive cakes—everyone's favorite—continue to be enjoyed as lapel pins or ring "stones."

PENDANT NECKLACES

Domino blocks, old keys, porcelain door escutcheons, medals, coins, small porcelain collectables—there are so many things you probably have squirreled away in cupboards and drawers that can be turned into pendants.

For the simplest and quickest projects, choose pendants with a central hole. If there's no hole, that's easy to rectify. Wooden jigsaw puzzle pieces, for example, can be converted using very small eye screws and a sharp bradawl. For items made of thin metal, make a hole with a fine hole punch; if the metal is slightly thicker, use a small drill bit. Then add a jump ring or a split ring. For the necklace, choose anything from discarded necklace and plumber's chains to ribbons and leather thongs.

WATCH FACE JEWELRY

Suddenly, there seems to be no end of interesting watch faces around, and they are very versatile. The large enamel ones look great as a single pendant hanging from a velvet ribbon or chain, connected by a jump ring, while eight assorted watch faces can make a really gorgeous bracelet (see page 35). We took three damaged multi-strand bracelets that we already had and joined them together with larger jump rings at the ends and also at three or four staggered points on the bracelets. You won't notice these connections and, in fact, you can add some of the watch faces to them as well—dual purpose! The result is a totally original piece of jewelry. Very glam!

DANCING MEDAL SHOES

When we came across a collection of medals for ballroom dancing, Latin American, tap and the like, we just had to find a project for them—they were far too special and unusual to ignore. So a bright idea struck us to use them on a pair of simple black shoes, a little like tap shoes, that would be well suited to dancing.

These medals were a particularly lucky find but you could try anything of a similar size—let your imagination run riot! Simply attach the items to the front of the shoes using epoxy glue, making sure they are correctly aligned and well stuck on, and allow them to dry thoroughly before dancing.

EARRING KEEPERS

Earrings have a terrible habit of disappearing. This might not be a problem if they are cheap and easily replaceable but it really does matter if they have sentimental value.

Keeping earrings in single boxes takes up too much space, and big jewelry boxes behave just like a large handbag—you simply can't find anything in them. So, we came up with this simple, space-saving idea of fitting small earrings through the holes of old vintage buttons and using the earring backs to hold them in place. Another idea is to make holes in a decorative playing card with a small hole punch, and group your earrings together. Old photographs can be used as a more personalized alternative, and are an unusual way of giving earrings as a gift. Hatpins and brooches can also be kept safe pinned through cards and photographs.

simple LAPEL PINS FROM EPAULETS

Old epaulets are such beautifully made items, always detailed with metallic braids or felt. Often found in army surplus stores and flea markets, they are normally full of lint (fluff) and need a good pressing, but once you have cleaned them up, a pair can make two original lapel pins, such as this Pony Club Rosette and Fishtail Badge.

For the Pony Club Rosette, you need one epaulet and about a yard (meter) of two or three complementary trims, such as rickrack, ribbon, and fine metallic braid—they just need to have body to them so they hold their shape. The middle of the rosette could be a round rhinestone brooch, a large bottle cap—in fact, any round and flat decorative item.

Decide how large you want your pin. Make loose loops with each of your trims, stitching them together in the center. Cut your epaulet into two even lengths. Fan them into two tails and stitch your rosette of trims securely to the top of the tails. Stitch a brooch back to the reverse. Dab some white glue over the trim stitching and cover with your chosen decorative middle. Make an angled or a fishtail cut to both tails, attach the lapel pin to a coat or jacket, and proceed to the Winner's Circle!

For the Fishtail Badge, cut a single tail and a top piece from the epaulet. Cut a piece of lightweight card just smaller than your top piece and glue it onto the back, to stiffen it, folding over the edges of the top piece. Stitch the tail to the top piece. Cover the card by gluing on a small piece of dark felt. Stitch on a brooch back. Cut a fishtail on the "ribbon." For decoration, try small pins, dancing medals, decorative buttons, even a coin.

simple
TAPE MEASURE
ROSETTE

Well-worn fabric tape measures often turn up at flea markets, and this rosette brooch is an original way to make use of them.

Cut the two hanging "ribbons" first, to a length you like, then form the rosette from the central section of ribbon left, looping the ribbon over and stitching as you go to hold it in place. Finish with a small central loop. If you are short on ribbon at the end, add a button, badge, or covered button for the middle. Stitch the ribbon ends onto the back of the rosette, followed by a brooch back.

simple
MEMORIES
ON A STRING

All of us have little things tucked away in drawers that bring back special memories when we come across them. This project brings them all together.

Tie on jump rings at roughly 2 in (5 cm) intervals along a length of silk string. As you find your small treasures, attach each one to a ring. If an item has no natural hanger, fix a jump ring to it with Superglue or epoxy glue. Tie in larger jump rings at each end of the string and hang them from small screw hooks in the walls.

Chapter Two
FABRICS AND TRIMS

step-by-step LACE DOILY LAMPSHADE

This is a fantastic project to recreate a lampshade using old lace doilies. Almost any kind of shade and lampstand will be suitable. Doilies come in a wide range of patterns and sizes. Mixed together on your shade, they will look gorgeous.

☞ MATERIALS:

Wire lampshade

Lamp base

Good supply of lace doilies—large, medium, and small

Iron

Pins

Needle and thread

Scissors

1 Strip your lampshade of the existing fabric. If there is binding tape on the wire that still looks white(ish!), there's no problem leaving it on. Otherwise, remove it.

2 Sort through the doilies, discarding any that are stained. Press the remainder with a cool iron. A mix of whites and creams works well together, or you could stay with the one color.

3 Starting with the largest of your doilies, pin one on the top of the frame, folding over just enough to secure with a pin. Pull down to the bottom of the frame and fold over to pin in place. If your doilies are much larger than the frame, you can sometimes use them diagonally. Repeat all the way around the frame. There will be large gaps but don't worry— you can fill these in with smaller doilies. Once the

large doilies are pinned in place, whipstitch them onto the top of the frame first, then the bottom.

4 Pin the medium-sized doilies to the upright struts of the frame, as well as to the large doilies underneath them. Sew them into place, attaching to the frame wherever possible. Finish with the smallest doilies, filling in the few remaining gaps that there will inevitably be. Replace the shade on your lamp base.

There is a
fair amount of
handstitching
required for
this project
but it's all
very easy!

Combining a rather thick wooly trim
with a more conventional silky fringe
gives just the right amount of wow
factor for this project.

step-by-step SILK SCARF LAMPSHADE

Even though traditional floor lamps have had something of a renaissance recently, they are still relatively easy to find in thrift stores (charity shops) and at flea markets. Re-covering the original shade is not difficult but it does require a degree of pinning and handstitching. Although not quick work, it can be done with one eye on the TV! Silk scarves that you no longer wear can make gorgeous lampshades but they do need to be lined to diffuse the light of the bulb.

☞ **MATERIALS:**

Standard lamp with shade

Tape measure

Paper, for the pattern

Pencil

White or cream cotton calico or sheeting, for the lining

Scissors

Sewing machine

Silk scarves

Pins

Needle and thread

Trim, for the top of the shade

White glue

Trim and wooly fringe, for the base of the shade

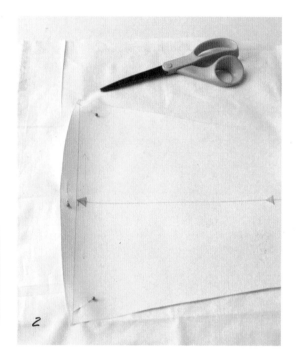

1 Remove the existing fabric from the lampshade. Measure the frame, including the circumference of the top and base of the shade. Check if the shade has a nipped-in waist and possibly a scalloped base—these details are important in determining the shape and size of the panels to be cut.

2 Draw a paper pattern for one panel, matching it to the shade. Enlarge the pattern to take into account any curves, and add at least 1 in (2.5 cm) top and bottom for turning under and securing to the frame, as well as a seam allowance of ½ in (1 cm) to each side of the panel. Lay out the paper pattern on the lining fabric and cut out as many panels as you have allowed.

3 Machine-stitch them together, leaving the last panel open so that you can check the lining will fit.

4 Pin the pattern to each of the scarves in turn, making sure that the pattern designs run in the same direction. Stitch the silk panels together, leaving the last part open as before. Lay the stitched silk fabric panels over the lining panels with wrong sides together. Pin and baste (tack) the panels together at the top edge.

5 Place the combined panels over the outside of the lampshade frame and secure with pins. The easiest way to do this is to start pinning at the top so you get the correct position, then securing the bottom in place and, finally, the sides. If your shade has a waist, pull the fabric to fit as you pin the sides—you may need to trim the fabric panels to ensure a neat fit. Make any fine adjustments after this point at the top of the shade.

6 Handstitch the panels in place at the top and the bottom inside the frame where the stitching won't be visible.

It's a good idea to cut out the lining first, as any adjustments you might have to make will be done on the less expensive and more replaceable cotton fabric.

7 Pin the trim to the wooly fringe, then secure with a long back stitch.

8 Pin the trim to the top of the shade, then glue into position. Remember to fold over the end so it will not fray. Any stitches in the panel will now be hidden by the trim.

9 Pin the combined trim to the base of the shade, making sure you follow the contours of the lampshade base to get the right curves. Secure into place with stitches or glue.

inspiration
SILK SCARF CUSHION

Vintage silk scarves are practical yet glamorous, with entire books having been written on the history of their design. Many of us have a collection of silk scarves tucked away somewhere but we probably only ever wear two or three of them. If we don't wear them, then why not use them in another way, so that they can be appreciated by others as well as ourselves?

To ensure your cushions enjoy a long life, use the best-quality scarves and check for signs of wear, which might cause the cushion to rip over time. Applying soft, lightweight iron-on interfacing to the reverse of the scarf is a good idea, to minimize creasing and give support to the fine silk.

The armchair here has been re-upholstered in Japanese denim with an assortment of old military buttons. These make a really interesting alternative to traditional covered buttons.

Souvenir scarves feature some of the most elegant designs and are certainly best appreciated when shown flat. They make the most incredible cushions and you can even build up a themed collection.

step-by-step PATCHWORK CUSHION

We're always finding needlepoints among old linens and other fabrics at flea markets but as no one seems to want them, they are invariably cheap to buy. A fantastic way to give them the prominence they deserve is to transform them into patchwork cushions.

☞ **MATERIALS:**

Tape measure

Cushion pad

Remnant fabrics, such as velvet, tweed, or wool

Piece of needlepoint

Scissors

Pins

Sewing machine

Iron

Zipper, almost the length of one side of the cushion

Tailor's chalk

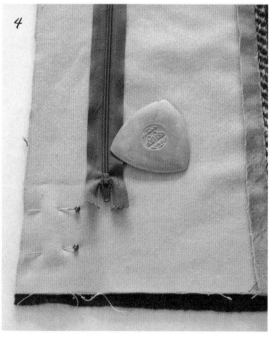

1 Measure the cushion pad to determine the size of patchwork required and note the measurements.

2 Choose fabric pieces that complement the colors and style of the needlepoint. Cut them into squares or rectangles, then pin together to make a front panel slightly larger than the cushion pad. Remember to include a ½ in (1 cm) seam allowance around each piece. Arrange the pieces so that the needlepoint is in the best position to be viewed.

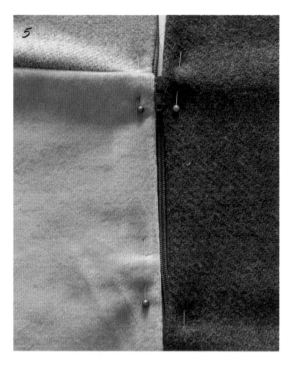

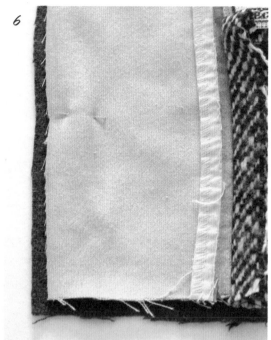

3 Stitch the fabric pieces together and press the seams flat.

4 For the back of the cushion, cut out a single piece of plain fabric the same size as the front panel. Place the front panel over the back piece, right sides together. Place the zipper toward the top edge of the back piece and mark the edge with tailor's chalk where the zipper ends. Pin and stitch the seam with a ½ in (1 cm) seam allowance.

5 Press the seam open and place the zipper under the turned-in edges. Pin and stitch the seam to secure the zipper in place. Press flat. Leave the zipper partly open at the end.

6 Place the wrong sides together and stitch the remaining three sides to make the cover. Open the zipper and turn the cushion cover inside out. Place the pad inside.

Needlepoints are often beautifully designed and skillfully made, so it's lovely to reinvent them as part of a cushion.

step-by-step
DOILY CURTAIN

There is a good reason why doilies were once so popular—they are both useful and versatile. You can pick them up very cheaply at flea markets. We have used them to decorate curtain panels made from vintage cotton sheets. The very fine cobweb doilies also look great appliquéd on sheer panels (top right).

☞ **MATERIALS:**

Tape measure

Old cotton sheet

Scissors

Iron

Pins

Sewing machine

Curtain header tape

Assorted lace doilies, plain or hand-dyed

Needle and thread (optional)

Curtain hooks and rings or other suitable fixing

---

1 Measure the window drop and add on sufficient length to allow for the bottom hem and the turning at the top. Cut the sheet to this measurement. If you can use the existing hem on the sheet, then it makes sense to do so. If not, make the bottom hem first by folding under ½ in (1 cm), pressing, then turning under at least 1–2 in (2.5–5 cm), depending on how much fabric you have to use. Pin, then stitch into place.

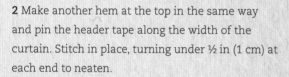

2

4

2 Make another hem at the top in the same way and pin the header tape along the width of the curtain. Stitch in place, turning under ½ in (1 cm) at each end to neaten.

3 Place the doilies on the curtain, mixing up the shapes, patterns, and colors to show them to best effect. Pin in place. You can then either handstitch them in place or use a sewing machine. Small doilies can be stitched just around the edges, but larger ones may require additional stitching in the middle so that they hold their shape when the curtains are hung up.

4 Attach curtain hooks and gather up the curtain using the strings in the header tape. Hang with curtain hooks on rings, or use whatever existing fixing you may have.

step-by-step HANDKERCHIEF SACHETS

Lavender sachets have a timeless appeal and make wonderful gifts, while beautiful embroidered (or printed) handkerchiefs are perfect for the task. These delightfully old-fashioned items, which no one seems to use anymore, crop up all the time at sales, often in gift boxed sets with the handkerchiefs in mint condition.

☞ **MATERIALS:**
Embroidered or printed hankerchief

Iron

Muslin

Sewing machine

Lavender flowers

Teaspoon

Needle and thread

Pins

Scissors

Button or other small decoration

1 Press the handkerchief. Place it so you are looking at a diamond, printed side down. Fold into an envelope by taking the right corner and folding it two-thirds into the handkerchief. Fold the left corner to the opposite side, so the triangles overlap, and then press. Fold the bottom corner up to make a pocket. Fold the top down to make a pointed front flap. Press again.

2 To make the inner bag, cut out a square of muslin that will fit snugly inside the handkerchief bag when it is filled with lavender flowers. Include a ½ in (1 cm) seam all around. Fold in half and stitch along the two open sides, leaving the top open. Spoon the flowers into the muslin bag.

3 Fold in the top seam on the sachet, pin, and handstitch to close. Place the sachet inside the handkerchief. To seal the envelope and secure the open front part of the envelope, handstitch a button or other small decoration on the point of the front flap, catching the pointed front flap and the two sides where they join as you stitch to retain the sachet shape.

Instead of a button, finish your
handkerchief lavender sachet with
a flourish, using a tiny medal,
silver bell, or jewelry charm.

step-by-step KNITTED FLOWER BROOCHES

We aren't the world's greatest knitters but even we can manage to make the simple knitted flower petals used in this brooch. As long as you remember to increase and decrease in the center of the petals, you shouldn't really go wrong.

☞ **MATERIALS:**

Size 2 (2.75 mm) knitting needles

4-ply knitting yarn (wool) in assorted colors

Large darning needle

Fabric remnants, such as printed cottons, tweed, and velvet

Pencil

Sharp scissors

Sewing machine

Needle and thread

Pretty button or small beads, for the flower center

Brooch back

1 To knit the petals, cast on 2 stitches, then knit 1 row. Continue in stockinette (stocking) stitch (knit 1 row, purl 1 row), increasing an extra stitch in the middle of every row so you gain 1 new stitch per row. Continue until you have 10 stitches. Work 3 rows even (straight) without increasing. Start decreasing (k2tog) from the center of each row so that you end up with a petal shape tapered at both ends. Bind (cast) off, leaving a long end of yarn. Your petal should be between 2 and 2½ in (5 and 7 cm) long.

2 Knit a further four or five petals, as preferred.

3 Neaten off all the petals by stitching the ends of the yarn into the back of the petals with the darning needle so the knitting is neat and the ends are nicely curved.

4 To make the fabric flower, draw a five-petaled flower shape with a pencil on a piece of remnant fabric—this should be approximately 4–5 in (10–13 cm) in diameter to suit the length of your knitted petals. You want the petals to come just to the edges of the fabric flower or slightly overlap when they are stitched in place. Repeat on a contrasting piece of fabric. Cut out both flower shapes with sharp scissors.

5 With a sewing machine, zigzag stitch all around the edge of the petals to neaten.

6 With right sides uppermost, place one fabric flower petal shape over the top of the other, very slightly offset so that the contrasting fabric underneath is visible. Arrange the knitted petals to fan out from the middle of the fabric flower. With the needle and thread, handstitch them in place in the middle of the flower, catching in all the yarn ends.

7 Sew on the button to make the flower center. Take your thread to the back and sew on a brooch back in the middle of the reverse of the flower to complete.

step-by-step
FABRIC REMNANT BROOCHES

What makes these brooches so special are the cigarette card "silks." In the first half of the last century, cigarette manufacturers included cards in their packs, for collecting in specially designed albums. Images of movie stars, flowers, and ocean liners were among the extraordinary illustrations now preserved as souvenirs of a lost time. The silks, which were produced in limited numbers, were made on a satin-type fabric printed with the collection design and laminated on card.

☞ MATERIALS:

Thin card from packaging box

Scissors

Cigarette card silk or piece of embroidery

Pinking shears

Pins

Jacquard ribbon

Fabric pieces, such as velvet or needlecord for the front of the brooch

Sewing machine

Toothpick or spatula

White glue

Piece of blanket, wool, or felt for the back of the brooch

Brooch back

Needle and thread

1 Choose the size for your finished brooch, then cut out a piece of card and a piece of velvet to match. Cut around the cigarette card silk with pinking shears for a decorative edge. Pin the silk to the jacquard ribbon. Pin the ribbon and silk to the piece of velvet for the front. Machine-stitch around the silk and along the sides of the ribbon.

2 Lay the velvet right side down and place the card on top, lining it up with the silk on the other side. Fold the long sides of the fabric and, using a toothpick, glue to the card at the back. Cut the four corners of the velvet to reduce the bulk and fold the two remaining sides down over the card, gluing behind to secure.

3 Cut out a piece of blanket slightly smaller than the back of the brooch, so that it will not show from the front. Handstitch the brooch back to the blanket. Glue the blanket to the back of the brooch.

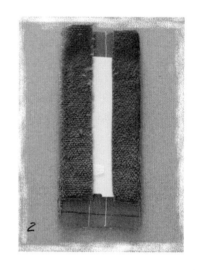

Keep an eye out for vintage jacquard ribbons, as well as cigarette silks. Their intricate patterns create just the right look for these pretty handmade brooches.

step-by-step DENIM JACKET DECORATION

Few people these days find the time to embroider but it was once an incredibly popular pastime. As a result, you will come across a lot of embroidered textiles at flea markets and in secondhand stores, often in mint condition. They make a fantastic decoration on the back of a plain denim jacket. Embroidered tablecloths or tray cloths will be about the right size, but make sure they are in tip-top condition.

☞ **MATERIALS:**
Vintage embroidered textile, such as a tablecloth or tray cloth

Small, sharp scissors

Denim jacket

Pins

Needle and thread

Old cotton lace

Inspiration

A quick and easy way to personalize a denim jacket is to hook a crochet flower over a front pocket button through the hole in the center of the flower. For our jacket, we also knitted leaves in yarn (wool) and handstitched them directly onto the denim.

1 Cut carefully around the embroidered area, making sure you leave all the stitching intact, and remove as much of the original base cloth as possible, to reveal just the embroidered part. The embroidery will not come apart if you don't cut into the stitching.

2 Lay the embroidery over the back of the jacket. Pin, then handstitch all around the piece—it should be sufficient to stitch only the outer edge, to hold the decoration in place.

3 To make the lovely lacy turn-up cuff, use old cotton lace of a depth to suit the cuff of your sleeve. Measure the width of the cuff and add on ½ in (1 cm) each end for turning a small hem. Cut the lace accordingly. Pin, then handstitch in place.

step-by-step
DISHTOWEL BAG

Traditional dishtowels have a simplicity of design and pattern that is well suited to other roles. So, if you find a collection of vintage or even modern dishtowels that takes your fancy, this is one easy sewing project for making use of them. A dishtowel bag is ideal for carrying a few small essentials around town or for storing household items, or as a handy lingerie or jewelry bag when traveling.

☞ MATERIALS:
Large dishtowel

Scissors

Tape measure

Webbing belt

Iron-on interfacing

Iron

Sewing machine

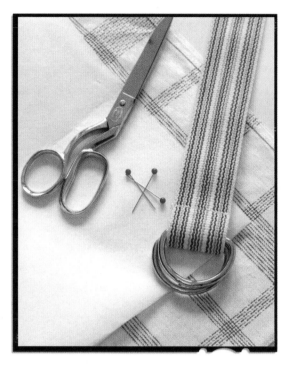

1 Cut off the hems of the dishtowel. Cut out a 6½ x 2 in (16 x 5 cm) rectangle from one end of the dishtowel for the handle loop and put to one side. Level off the dishtowel, then cut the remainder in half for the bag and the lining. Cut a 16½ in (42 cm) length of webbing from the belt.

2 Cut out a piece of interfacing that measures slightly less all around than the lining. Press it into place on the lining.

3 Fold the bag rectangle in half sideways, then do the same with the lining, with the interface on the outside. Pin, then stitch along the two sides of both rectangles to make bag shapes. Trim the seams.

4 Turn in a ½ in (1 cm) hem on the top edges of the bag and the lining. Press.

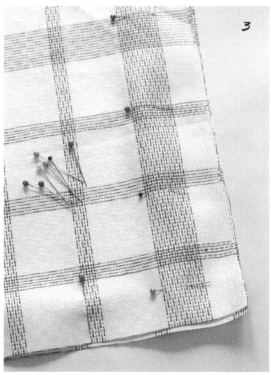

Unused linen dishtowels are surprisingly simple to find
and the fabric is a joy to sew, being so crisp
and easy to work with. You can achieve a surprisingly
professional finish on this quick project.

5 Press the fabric under ¼ in (5 mm) on each long side of the loop piece. Then fold it in half and press again to enclose all the raw edges inside. Fold the length of webbing in half across the width to form the strap.

6 Turn the bag rectangle right side out. Place the lining inside so that the interface is up against the bag.

7 Pin the loop piece in position between the bag and the lining at the center point of the top of the bag. Make sure the loop is pointing outward and is placed so that the webbing strap will fit through the loop. Place the folded webbing opposite the loop to form a strap.

8 Pin the lining to the bag and stitch all around the top, securing the loop and the webbing strap in place.

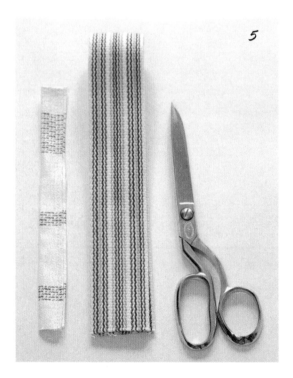

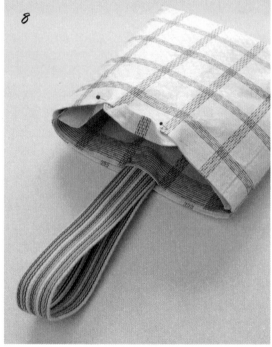

inspiration
MESSENGER BAG

Dishtowels come in so many designs and colors. We love the souvenir ones that were often purchased on vacations as a reminder of a family trip to the seaside. All too often these towels seem to have been put away unused, being considered just too special, and so they turn up in secondhand stores in pristine condition, which makes them perfect for making into simple projects.

This delightful messenger bag uses a vintage dishtowel found in a French junk shop. It depicts a rural scene and a calender of 1986, but you could easily find kitsch souvenirs of vacations much closer to home, or even a collection of elegant roses or nautical knots and symbols. Have fun with whatever you find!

Easy to make, the bag is sewn with a plain cotton lining and then finished with a leather belt strap made from two narrow belts buckled together. The strap is then attached with rings and fabric loops to the bag itself.

For heavier fabric bags, use a hole punch to cut five holes in the belts. Configure them like a five on a dice, then stitch with heavy button thread onto the bag.

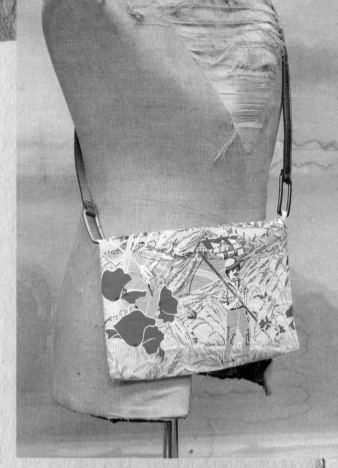

inspiration
DESIGNER BAG

Look closely and you should be able to see that this stunning shoulder bag has been assembled from a lady's suit jacket.

It's possible to make bags
from all sorts of items
that you probably already
own but no longer use or
wear, and decorate them
with all manner of trims,
ribbons, and tassels.

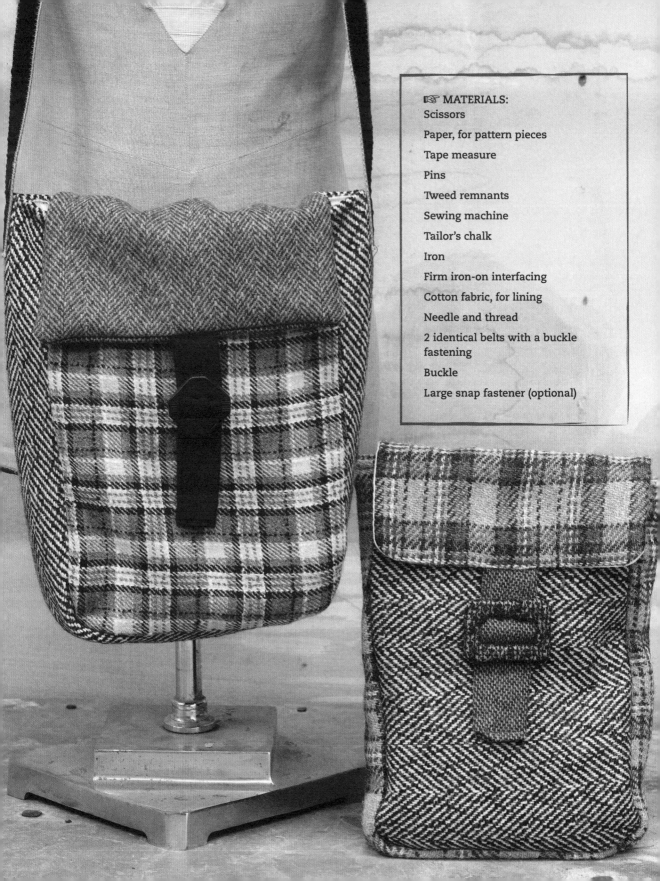

☞ MATERIALS:
Scissors

Paper, for pattern pieces

Tape measure

Pins

Tweed remnants

Sewing machine

Tailor's chalk

Iron

Firm iron-on interfacing

Cotton fabric, for lining

Needle and thread

2 identical belts with a buckle fastening

Buckle

Large snap fastener (optional)

step-by-step TWEED LAPTOP BAG

Using remnants of hardwearing tweed, we created our own bespoke laptop bag. It's up to you how big you make it—it can be a snug fit or roomy so that it will hold all your laptop accessories as well. Our laptop was small, 11½ x 8½ in (29 x 22 cm), but the following measurements can be adapted for different sizes.

1 Cut out paper patterns to the following measurements:
Front panel: 11 x 14½ in (28 x 36 cm)
Back panel (including flap): 20 x 10 in (50 x 25 cm)
Side band: 4 x 36½ in (10 x 91 cm)
Inside flap backing: 10 x 6 in (25 x 15 cm)

2 Pin the patterns to the tweed and cut out.

3 Reinforce the base of the front tweed panel by machine-stitching along the seam allowance ½ in (1 cm) from the edge of the bottom and around the corners, extending the stitching to 2 in (5 cm) above each corner. Mark with tailor's chalk the position of the side band on the back panel—this should be 6½ in (16 cm) below the top of the back flap. Pin the side band from this point all around, then stitch.

4 Pin the front panel to the side band. Clip the corners to ease the front into the band, then stitch together.

5 Check the width required for the front strap. Double it and add 1 in (2.5 cm) for turning in each side. Cut out in tweed. Fold each turning, press, and fold in half. Stitch through all the thicknesses.

6 Pin the front strap to the inside of the flap at its center point. With right sides together, pin the flap backing to the flap, matching the top and sides. Stitch and turn the right way out.

7 Cut out two pieces of firm iron-on interfacing measuring 2 x 1½ in (5 x 4 cm). Apply the strips to each side panel at the top. This will reinforce where the shoulder strap is to go.

4

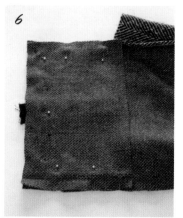

6

14

8 To make the lining, cut out one piece of cotton fabric to the same size as the pattern for the front tweed panel, one piece to the same size as the back panel (minus flap), and one piece to the same size as the side band.

9 To make the pockets, cut out in tweed one piece measuring 7 x 4 in (17 x 10 cm) and a second measuring 5 x 6 in (13 x 15 cm). Turn under a ½ in (1 cm) seam allowance all around and press. Stitch the top edge to finish the hem.

10 Pin the pockets to the back lining of the bag with the wrong side facing the right side of the fabric. Stitch on three sides, leaving the top open.

11 Pin and stitch the side band of the lining to the front and back (as before for the tweed) to complete the lining. Fold under and press a ½ in (1 cm) seam allowance at the top edge, along the top of the lining bag. Press.

12 With wrong sides together, pin the lining inside the bag with the turned-under hem along the inner edge. Stitch around the front and side panels. Do not stitch the back. Fold the backing of the flap over the lining and handstitch in place.

13 To make the shoulder strap, join the two belts together through one of their buckles. Measure the length required for the belt to cross the body. Mark with tailor's chalk and cut off the excess, which will include the buckle of one belt.

14 Pin each end of the shoulder strap to the sides of the bag over the reinforced area. Stitch together using the leather needle on your sewing machine. If the strap is too thick for your machine, take it to a shoe repairer to do the job for you.

15 Handstitch the buckle to the front of the bag so that the front strap can be threaded through it. Secure with a snap fastener, if required.

simple PHONE SLEEVE

A child's sweater makes a great cover for a cell phone, as the width of a sleeve is the perfect fit for most new-style phones. Once you have all the materials to hand, this project should take you no more than fifteen minutes.

A fun alternative to the sweater is an adult's sock!

Lay the phone on the sleeve, lining it up with the bottom of the ribbing. Mark where the other end of the phone sits with tailor's chalk. Cut the sleeve.

Check the phone will fit snugly inside the cut sleeve and not come out too easily. If the sleeve seems too wide, reduce its width by stitching a seam inside the existing seam to make the sleeve narrower. Turn the sleeve inside out and pin and stitch the open end. Turn the right way out.

inspiration
DYEING FABRICS

Dyeing—either by hand or in the washing machine—is a fantastic way to inject some color into your home and your wardrobe. It is really simple to do, takes very little effort, and the results are generally foolproof, as long as you follow the manufacturer's instructions that come with the dye. You may, though, be in for a few surprises, so take a laid-back attitude and see what comes out in the wash!

IT'S GOOD TO KNOW...

Hand-dyeing is best suited to small items such as shirts and smaller fabric pieces. You can also dye more delicate items such as lace and trims to use as appliqué on clothes and homewares, and also lace doilies, as featured in our Doily Curtain project (see pages 56–7). Constant stirring is required.

Cotton is the best material to dye because it takes the color so well. For the best results, stick to 100 percent cotton, linen, viscose, or high cotton-mix textiles. Generally, avoid dyeing wool and polyester. Bear in mind that polyester thread is often used in modern clothing and may dye to a lighter shade than the rest of the item.

Dyes will work well on white or light colors, or as a darker shade of an existing color. However, the shade of the original item will have a bearing on the end result, so always consider this when choosing a color.

Always weigh the item to be dyed, and check the weight of fabric that can be dyed per pack—you may need to buy more than one pack.

Ordinary table salt is an essential ingredient for all dyeing projects and, of course, so is water.

lease use this
achine for

EXTRA
TY WASHING

VERALLS etc

Machine-dyeing is really simple and takes very
little effort because the machine does most of the
work for you. You will, though, need to run the
machine through at least two wash cycles, which
means the process takes a little longer to complete.
You will also need to run the machine again after
dyeing to be sure it is free of color for future
washes. Try this option for larger items such as
curtains, tablecloths, and bedding.

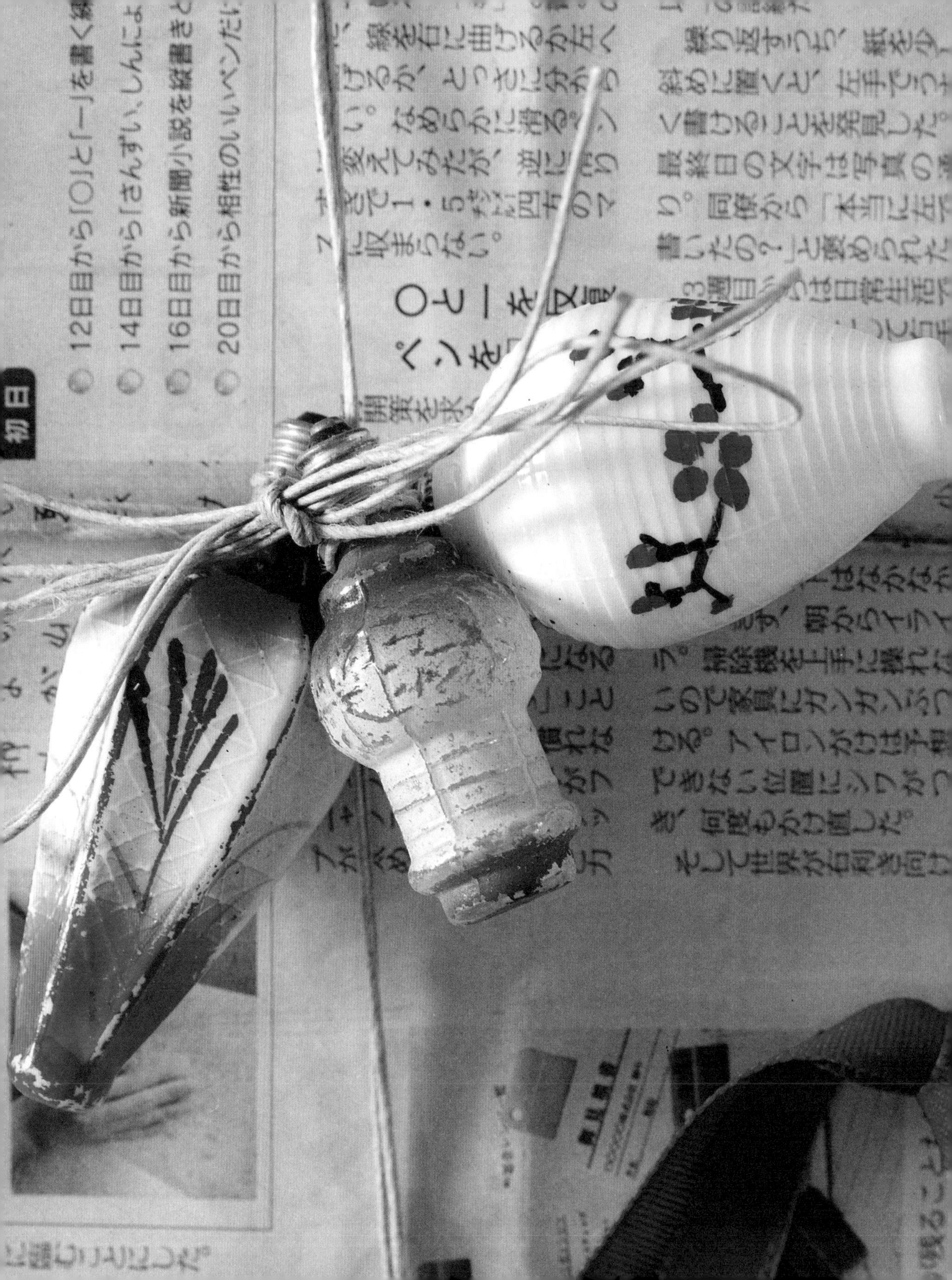

Chapter
Three

PAPER
AND
CARD

simple
PATCHWORK
WALLPAPER

Wallpapering just one small wall in a room or the inside of an alcove behind shelves, will add instant drama and excitement to a space.

The simplest way to wallpaper is to create a patchwork wall. You work with small, easy-to-manage pieces that don't have to match, overlap the paper, and you don't need to worry about a true plumb line as you would when working with regular paper. The only materials you need are wallpaper paste, made with water, and a work surface.

Start papering at a top corner and work down and across diagonally. You don't need to cover the entire wall as you go, just randomly cover the wall or area once, then go over it again with a second layer, filling in any gaps.

For inspiration, here are some examples of different papers—the older and more unusual they are, the more charming the effect—that can be used to make a patchwork wallpaper: sheet music, vintage gift wrap, pages from a book in a foreign language, vintage sewing pattern instructions, a flowering bulb catalog, and a vintage wallpaper sample book.

Sort your papers in advance, so you can give your favorite pieces pride of place.

Embroidery or needlepoint paper patterns are charming on a wall in a small space, like this shelved alcove.

simple DESIGNER ENVELOPES

Envelopes are remarkably useful things to have around, and making your own couldn't be simpler. They come in all sorts of shapes and sizes, from the tiny brown ones used traditionally for weekly pay packets, through to everyday white letter envelopes, to larger ones that are great for enclosing book pages or photographs. Then there are seed packets, airmail envelopes, and small notecards.

If you have a favorite style and shape of envelope, create a template, just like a paper sewing pattern, which you can use time and time again. Start with a bought envelope, peeling it apart carefully. Lay it flat on a piece of card, draw around it, then cut it out with a craft knife. Remember to mark the template, as you will probably be tempted to make more than one and you will want to remember which is which. Even better, glue the original envelope to the template so you will instantly recognize it. From there, you can start making your own unique envelopes.

Place the template onto the paper you have chosen for your envelope, draw around the outline with a pencil ,and then cut out the envelope shape with scissors or a craft knife. To make up the envelope, apply white glue or a glue stick along the previous glue lines and fold up the bottom and sides to secure the envelope. Press down all the edges to ensure they are well stuck.

Get into the habit of collecting used but unwrinkled gift wrap, book pages, leftover wallpaper, foreign newspapers, brown craft paper, maps, sheet music, sewing patterns, vintage magazines, newspapers, and catalogs. If some of the paper is a bit fragile,

you can always glue it to new, cheap printer paper so it will have more resilience. You can even use unwanted printed pages from your home computer that you would otherwise put in the recycling.

One lovely envelope project is making seed packets to hold seed that you have saved from your garden and giving them as gifts. You can either open up an existing seed packet and use it as a template or create a larger version, as we did.

For the outer envelope, cut out a rectangle of paper measuring 9½ x 6½ in (24 x 16 cm). We made a number of envelopes from recycled gift wrap in an assortment of patterns. Place the rectangle face down in landscape format (with the longest measurement at the bottom). Fold up ¼ in (5 mm) all along the width of the paper, which will become the bottom of the envelope. Glue in place with a glue stick and press down firmly.

Then make a crease in the paper 2½ in (6 cm) along from the left-hand side and fold to the center. Fold the right-hand side of the paper to the center, lapping over the left side by ½ in (1 cm) to make a seam. Glue the seam in place. You now have a wallet shape and two options for finishing.

The more decorative option is to simply punch a hole about 1 in (2.5 cm) from the top in the middle of the envelope. Thread a gift tag through the hole and inscribe your message or greeting. Brown luggage tags are excellent for this and look great with almost any style of printed paper. With this finish, you will also need to make a smaller envelope to go inside that will actually hold the seeds. Follow our envelope template idea above.

An alternative way of finishing the envelope is to add a flap to it. Draw a pencil line across one layer of the envelope, 1¼ in (3 cm) down from the open top. With sharp scissors, cut across the line and up the sides, leaving the second layer intact, which becomes the front flap. Cut the flap at an angle of 30 degrees on each side to form a tab, which you then fold to the back of the envelope. To secure the contents, you can either glue this tab or add a sticker. Larger vegetable seeds such as beans and peas won't need an additional inside envelope. Remember to mark on the envelope what seeds are contained inside and give some easy-to-follow growing instructions.

inspiration

Creative closures for your envelopes made from tabs, paper loops, buttons, and string are lovely decorative touches.

Cut out a small tab on the flap of the envelope—¼–½ in (5–10 mm) long should be about right. Glue a narrow band of paper across the envelope ¼ in (5 mm) deep and wide enough so that the tab can fit through it to secure the envelope flap. This works especially well for an envelope made from wallpaper, which is stiffer and more resilient. Attach a small button and loop, made of string. The loop can be glued to the underneath of the envelope flap, with an additional piece of paper over the ends of the string loop, while the button can be handstitched to the paper envelope. If the paper seems a little flimsy, paste a small extra piece behind where you intend to have the button and stitch through both thicknesses.

Another alternative is to have two buttons, one on the flap and one on the envelope itself, together with a long single piece of string that can be wound around both buttons in a figure eight.

simple INGENIOUS GIFT WRAP

When you have taken the time to choose the perfect gift, you really want to present it in the most tempting wrapping. With a little imagination, you can create the most stylish and individual gift wrap, which will save you money as well as a trip to the stores.

Try vintage wallpapers, sheet music, old maps, book pages, and foreign newspapers, especially those printed on colored paper, which look fantastic contrasted with fancy ribbon and trim decorations. Old sewing and knitting patterns make the most appropriate gift wrap for a creative crafting friend, especially when combined with a tag made from an

old yarn or a button card. Then there are vintage posters, which you can match to the recipient's interests, handwritten deeds, and old documents. If you find old birthday cards with a double fold, open them out and use to wrap small gifts, placing the design where it will be shown to best effect.

Our favorite brown craft paper is the best possible standby. Armed with some rubber stamps and colored ink pads, you can produce personalized gift wrap with it quickly and cheaply. Another option is

to cut out images from old books—children's annuals are a particular favorite—and glue these to the brown paper once you have wrapped the gift so you can place the chosen image to best effect. You can also make your own stencils from card and use them to make decorative designs, such as the recipient's initials or an appropriate motif, to personalize your gift.

Save the stamps on letters, particularly those from foreign countries, and decorate your parcels with them. As a variation on the theme, you can create your own stamp with a photograph or a magazine cut-out, embellished with some postage-style wavy lines across the image.

simple GIFT TRIMMINGS AND TAGS

Once you have wrapped your gift, complete the presentation with some decorative trimming, such as leftover yarn, ribbon, lace, string, even a shoelace, and a suitable gift tag. Making your own tags is a whole lot of fun.

Each tag takes only a small piece of recycled card or paper, and can be as individual as the recipient. Use your imagination to reuse all manner of cards and papers to make bespoke gift tags, from the obvious Christmas and birthday cards, through book illustrations, old paperback covers, vinyl record sleeves, yarn or button cards, to photo transparencies, vintage family photographs, playing cards, old paint-by-numbers and oil paintings.

Punch holes in the corners of old florist's cards, place settings, and business cards, then tie on tiny toys, a piece of broken jewelry for extra bling, or appropriately festive decorations. You can also use vintage buttons to secure string wrapped around a parcel by threading the twine through the button.

Vintage cigarette cards make wonderful gift tags. These little cards, so popular in the first half of the last century, are easy to find at flea markets. They are also very inexpensive. Given that the cards celebrate so many interests, you are sure to be able to find some to delight your friends and family.

Attach a cigarette card to some plain card, on which you can write your greeting, with string or ribbon threaded through a hole made with a hole punch. Cutting the paper with pinking shears gives a pretty decorative edge.

inspiration

Although not strictly a gift tag, a suitcase tag, to set your luggage apart from everyone else's, can be made by using part of an old oil painting (see picture page 86, far right). Cut two equal-sized pieces from the canvas. In the middle of one, cut out a window for your address card. Glue a piece of clear plastic from some gift packaging to the back of the window, to make a waterproof cover for the card. Position the card at the window and glue or machine-stitch the two pieces of canvas together, back to back. Make a thin strap with a simple buckle closure, such as you might find on a child's shoe. Create a slit in the top of the tag, thread the strap through, then through your suitcase handle.

We guarantee that the small amount of extra effort it takes to make your own tags will earn you a reputation as a gift wrapper par excellence!

simple NOTEBOOK AND PAPERS

It feels good to use a notebook that you have made yourself. We made ours with a pretty illustration from an old children's book on its cover. Alongside are all sorts of different papers that have been recycled into something new, from cigarette cards and sheet music to paint-by-numbers paintings and maps.

To make the pages, cut your paper to double the required size of the finished page—between 25 and 30 sheets should be about right. Fold each sheet in half widthwise and mark the center line with a pencil. Mark three holes along this line, roughly one in the center and the other two evenly spaced either side. Punch a hole through all thicknesses on each of the three penciled marks. Put to one side.

To make the cover, cut out a piece of card slightly larger than the unfolded pages you have already cut—½–¾ in (1–2 cm) larger all around is about right. Cut out a piece of fabric or decorative paper ½ in (1 cm) wider all around than the card. Apply white glue to one side of the card and stick the fabric or paper to it, adding more glue to the exposed fabric edge before turning in the sides and snipping the corners so you reduce the bulk of the fabric. This is the outside of the cover.

Glue a piece of plain paper to the inside to go over the card and onto the fabric edge, leaving a small border of fabric visible on the inside.

Choose a pretty image for the outside of the cover and glue in place. Place the pages inside and mark where the three corresponding cover holes should be made. Punch through the cover accordingly.

Thread a large darning needle with fine string, enough to wrap around the book several times, and knot the end. Stitch the cover and the pages together, starting in the middle hole with the knot on the inside. Follow a figure eight as you stitch through the holes, finishing with the string coming back through the middle hole to the outside. Fold the book shut. The string remaining can be wound around and tucked in to keep the notebook closed.

simple BIRTHDAY BUNTING

Many of us collect greetings cards that we have received over the years for various celebrations, such as important birthdays and anniversaries. You might also have kept hold of cards on behalf of your young children, or inherited old cards. Rather than storing them in a box or a drawer and forgetting all about them, why not turn them into colorful bunting for hanging up to celebrate new special occasions.

Cut each card into a pennant, with the apex of the triangle being the bottom of the pennant. Punch a hole about ½ in (1 cm) in from each corner of the shortest length.

String the cards onto string or ribbon, threading through the back of one, then through the front of the next, and so on. Leave a length of string or ribbon at each end for hanging your bunting.

simple CUPCAKE CASE GARLANDS

Paper cases for cupcakes and muffins make really unusual festive garlands. They are cheap and colorful and look amazing strung together. Even a mix of all shades of white cases looks brilliant, too! Making this project is so easy, you can do it while watching TV. During a movie, you can make yards of them—very satisfying!

Set out your papers in stacks of different patterns, colors, and sizes. Thread a mattress needle with yarn. These needles are almost 12 in (30 cm) long and are perfect for this job, while yarn holds the papers better than string or thread.

Thread the cases in a random order, one by one, onto the yarn, sometimes with the top of the cases touching, sometimes the other way around. This will give real volume and interest to your garlands, and the more random the order, the quicker you will be able to make them. Tie the ends off into a loop for hanging.

For long garlands, simply make smaller ones and tie them together. Alternatively, work from the middle of the yarn toward one end, tying off the yarn when you reach it. Repeat for the other end.

Whenever you bake muffins or cupcakes, save any leftover paper cases, and if you are treated to a box of chocolates, save their cases, too.

simple
CELEBRATION TABLE

**We always like to make a celebration really special and take time to decorate
the table in our own style, using of mix of vintage, handmade, and new.**

For this afternoon birthday tea, held in the
conservatory, we covered a rescued old garden
table with a damask tablecloth, which we had dyed
green (see Dyeing Fabrics, pages 76–9). The cloth
had seen better days but its new color rejuvenated
it. The six handstitched napkins, all different
patterns, were made into a new "set" by dyeing
them with the tablecloth. Don't worry if pieces take
the dye slightly differently—it all adds to the
character and the aged look. The chairs, which we

salvaged from dumpsters (skips) on the street, were
either painted with leftover paint or left just as we
found them, enhancing the eclectic look.

Our special 21st birthday bunting and cupcake case
garlands (see pages 92 and 93) hanging from the
ceiling add a personalized note to this celebration,
but there are so many other lovely kinds of paper
bunting you can make using your own memorabilia.

A homemade cake, always more special than a
bought one, was displayed on a cake stand made
from repurposed tart pans, upended on a silver
candlestick. Delicious meringues and other
tempting treats, meanwhile, were piled on a tiered
cake stand made from more tart pans on a
threaded metal rod (see pages 150–52).

We turned some delightful frilly-edged mini
lampshades upside down and used them as vases.
Simply line the inside of the shade with two small
plastic bags, one on either side of the wire frame, to
display your guest of honor's favorite flowers.

A collection of assorted molded and engraved glass
sundae dishes was pressed into service as pretty
containers for hand-poured candles. The patterned
china teacups, saucers, and plates, none of them
matching, convey the fun you can have collecting
whatever designs take your fancy. A complete set of
anything simply isn't necessary.

simple BUNTING FOR THE BOYS

This is really fun bunting for any kind of male celebration—leaving school, getting a new job or being promoted, retirement, a birthday—there are endless possibilities! It's also easy to fold up and store for the next occasion.

A collection of neckties is essential but we can more or less guarantee that once you mention to friends and family that you need some for a project, you will be inundated! If you're not, then thrift stores (charity shops) are a great source.

The best hanging "ribbon" to use is wide cotton seam binding, or hemming tape. It is usually about 1½ in (4 cm) wide, with a pressed edge on each side, which makes it ideal for this project. Cut the binding to the required length, allowing extra for hanging the bunting, then press it in half along its length with an iron.

Sort out your neckties, rejecting any that are too worn or stained. Cut each tie so that you have a pile of wide ends about 10 in (25 cm) long, and narrow ends about 6 in (15 cm) long. Mix up the patterns, then arrange the ends in pairs, back to back.

Starting at one end of your binding, pin in a pair of narrow ends and sew a straight line along the binding edges, securing the ties. Pin in and sew a pair of wide ends 2½–3 in (6–8 cm) further along on the binding. Continue like this with all your ties. If you have enough to complete the length you want, the bunting will be finished in no time.

For flag bunting made of thin paper, it's a good idea to reinforce each pennant with brown craft paper or recycled printer paper glued onto the back. Glue the paper on first, using a glue stick or rubber cement, then cut out the pennant shapes.

Playing cards, postcards, book pages, comics, and old photos all make delightful bunting. Cut them into pennants, like the greetings card bunting, punch holes in the top corners, and thread onto ribbon or string.

Chapter Four

CHINA
AND
WOOD

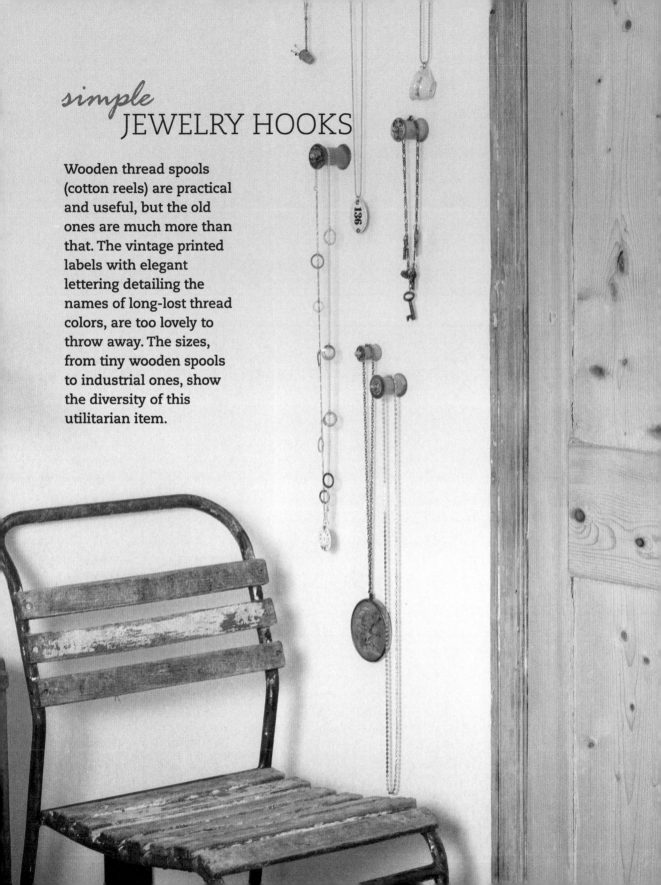

simple
JEWELRY HOOKS

Wooden thread spools (cotton reels) are practical and useful, but the old ones are much more than that. The vintage printed labels with elegant lettering detailing the names of long-lost thread colors, are too lovely to throw away. The sizes, from tiny wooden spools to industrial ones, show the diversity of this utilitarian item.

The double-ended screws you will need for this project are very specific. They have one end tapered and threaded to screw into the wall, with the other end smooth and cylindrical. There is no screw head, so the end needs to be covered. Match your screws to the width of the hole in each spool and the overall length, adding on an extra ½ in (1 cm), so that once the screw is in the wall, there is enough of it protruding for the top nut to be screwed onto it.

Work out where you would like to position each spool, and mark with a pencil. Drill a hole with an electric drill, and plug it with a suitable wall anchor (Rawlplug). Position the screw through the hole in the spool and screw to the wall securely through the wall anchor. Finish off the hooks neatly by adding the correct size of domed top nut to fit the screw.

Practical and lovely to look at, these spools are a great way to store necklaces and bracelets, happily in full view!

simple WOODEN DRAWER PULLS

Wooden thread spools (cotton reels) make really practical drawer pulls. For each one, you will need a straight cylinder screw and a domed top nut. The screw will need to be the length of your spool added on to the depth of the drawer front, with a little extra length on top to allow for screwing on the top nut. These come in both brass and nickel—choose the color you like best!

inspiration

Tiny thread spools (cotton reels), still wound with colorful thread, make very sweet holders for birthday cake candles, while two metal tart pans in graduated sizes, stacked one on top of the other, make a gorgeous cake stand—and there's no need for any permanent fixing!

Try to find screws that just fit through the diameter of the spools, to make the final fit that much better. Drill a hole in the drawer front to the same diameter as the spool, and place a screw in the hole from inside the drawer. Add the spool, with the attractive paper end to the front, then the top nut, and tighten, to secure in place. All done!

inspiration

Thread spools make easy-to-grip knobs on
vintage tins. Simply drill a hole in the
middle of the lid and attach the spool as for
the Drawer Pull.

simple
CERAMIC DOORKNOB HOOKS

Ceramic doorknobs make attractive and convenient storage solutions for all manner of things. We decided to hang ours in a walk-in closet to tidy away baskets that used to lie all over the floor. Choosing the motifs for the knobs is a huge amount of fun—we cut out numbers from a calligraphy paperback. Once you have assembled all the materials, this project should take less than thirty minutes.

Choose an electric drill bit and wall anchor (Rawlplug) to fit the size of the screw in the back of the doorknob. Mark the desired position of the knob on the wall with a pencil, then drill a hole and plug it. Once you have secured the knob, you can add the number or other chosen motif. Cut around the motif with scissors, glue the back of the paper, and place it in position on the doorknob. Resist the temptation to do this before the knob is in place, as the motif might end up facing the wrong way!

The ceramic doorknobs for this project must have a screw coming out of the back. Knobs with a flat end and a wing nut are not suitable.

Letters and numbers in decorative
fonts make lovely personalized motifs.

step-by-step TEAPOT PINCUSHION

We come across so many cute items perfect for turning into pincushions. You could use the china from a child's tea service, a demitasse cup, an old silver eggcup... the possibilities are endless. Here, we've given instructions using an old tin child's teapot but they are the same for almost anything. The best items are either cylindrical in shape or nipped in at the top because the pincushion will sit in them securely. The project starts with a traditional tomato pincushion—we recommend that whenever you see one of these for sale at the right price, you buy it. If you don't have one, simply add sand and sawdust to the list of materials below, and use roughly one part sand to two parts sawdust.

☞ **MATERIALS:**
Scissors

Traditional tomato pincushion

Plate, for emptying the tomato pincushion

Old tin child's teapot

Old white handkerchief or part of an unworn white T-shirt

Two lengths of old ribbon, seam binding, or old shoe laces, or similar, each measuring about 6 in (15 cm) long

Decorative handkerchief or similar-sized piece of cloth, woven or knitted

Glue, white or transparent

Toothpick (optional), for spreading glue under the rim

Pins

Most old pincushions will have needles and pins inside, so be careful as you sort through the sand.

1 Cut a hole in the tomato pincushion and pour the contents gently onto the plate. Sort through the sand very carefully to remove any needles and pins. Save these for future projects. Once you are free of them, proceed!

2 Pour some sand from the plate into the old white handkerchief and gather it in the center. Twist the ends of the handkerchief together to make a ball and secure it with one of the ribbons. Trim the ribbon ends. Push the ball gently into the teapot to test for size—it should be a good tight fit but still go through the opening. Adjust the amount of sand in the handkerchief until the fit is right.

3 Cover the white handkerchief with the decorative handkerchief and secure it with the second ribbon. Test the ball for size in the teapot. If there is too much fabric to fit inside the teapot, trim some off from the ends.

4 Dab a small amount of glue evenly around the inside rim of the teapot. Ease the ball gently into place. When about halfway in and fitting snugly, let the glue set. If more glue is needed, very carefully insert a little more around the rim with a toothpick.

step-by-step CERAMIC PLANT MARKERS

It feels good to be able to repurpose something you have accidentally broken. Instead of throwing away cracked and smashed cups, plates, and saucers, try using them in new ways. This project reinvents them as plant markers for the garden.

☞ MATERIALS:

Broken china

Small hammer

Protective gloves and goggles

Coarse sandpaper

Epoxy glue

Spatula

Popsicle (lolly) stick

Permanent marker pen

1 Tap around the edges of the piece of china you want to use with a small hammer—make sure that you wear protective gloves and goggles, as flying china can be very sharp and dangerous! Look for areas with pretty decorations, such as flowers or geometric borders, and also with a clear space on which you can write the plant name. A triangular shape works the best, with the words written along one of the edges. For this reason, plate or saucer rims are the preferred option because you already have a smooth, curved edge.

2 Once you have some shapes that you like, rub down the sides with coarse sandpaper, to eliminate the sharp edges. Mix the epoxy glue and spread it on the china with a spatula. Then place a wooden popsicle (lolly) stick on the glue and allow to dry completely. Make sure the stick is level so that the china will set straight.

3 When completely dry, write the plant name on the china using a permanent marker pen and place the marker in the plant pot.

You are sure to have some pieces of china left over that you don't intend to use as plant markers. Rather than throw them away, give them something useful to do as top-dressing for pot plants. Not only will the china look very pretty but it will also prevent weeds taking hold and slow down water evaporation, meaning less watering.

Keep a jar to hand for bits of broken china. Once you rub down the edges, they make great labels for homemade preserves as well. Glue them to ribbon and tie on.

simple
TUREEN CANDLE

We chose a tureen to make this candle but could have used drinking glasses, teacups, glass bowls, and all manner of recycled food and gift cans. By adding some essential oils, you can create your own special scents to enjoy in addition to the lovely candlelight.

Candles are easy to make at home but you must always follow the manufacturer's instructions because you are working with hot wax, which can cause serious injury if not handled properly. All the materials you will need—candle wax, wicks (for a large container like a tureen, you will need between three and five for the candle to burn correctly), and cores—can be bought from a candle-making supplier, who should be able to give you help and advice on all aspects of candle-making.

inspiration

Old tins often have the most beautiful printed designs on their lids. However, sometimes the metal can be a little too rusted that you're at a loss as to what to do with them. If that's the case, why not use the tin as a container for a candle instead and take it on your travels? For a small tin, you should be able to make the candle in one pour of wax.

simple
TUREEN LID BIRD FEEDERS

If your tureen lid has a loop-type handle on the top, you might even be able to hang further treats from it, such as apples on skewers (see below). Position the lid in a tree, hook an "S" hook through the treats, then hang it from the handle.

inspiration

Sometimes the apples you buy just don't taste great or they get overlooked in the fruit bowl and become soft and wrinkly. You might not fancy eating them but the birds will! Simply push a long metal skewer through the center of each apple and add a cork on the end. Hook the loop end of the skewer onto a length of sturdy chain to hang through a tree.

This project is an ingenious way of using a spare tureen lid. Glazed lids are very easy to wash and keep clean. Metal saucepan lids work equally well.

Simply place the tureen lid upside down securely between the branches of a tree or a climber, then fill it with an assortment of bird treats—nuts, seeds, fat balls, and so on—to make a decorative as well as useful feeder.

simple TUREEN PLANTERS

Tureens make charming planters for small spring-flowering bulbs, with narcissi, muscari, crocus, iris, and snowdrops all perfect candidates. Bulbs need only a fairly shallow space in which to grow, and as long as you don't overwater the plants, they will do fine and look delightful. Place them indoors or by your front door, or on a patio or a terrace.

If the tureen is fairly deep, place some grit or gravel at the bottom before adding the potting soil (compost)—this will prevent the potting soil from becoming waterlogged. Why not plant one up as a gift and place a ceramic plant marker (see pages 108–10) inside inscribed for the recipient?

We like to use moss or even some small and pretty garden weeds on the soil surface so the planting looks more natural and you avoid that "just planted" look. Shards of broken china make great topdressing. If you are planting up a larger tureen or container, add a little grass seed to the soil. Old colanders are ideal plant containers, with their holes providing perfect drainage. Indoors, place your containers on a large platter to display. Outdoors, they can stand directly on a table or on the patio/terrace.

For smaller displays, plant up gravy boats. Tiny bulbs look beautiful on their own in tiny teacups, on their saucers.

Chapter Five

GLASS AND MIRROR

simple LACE GLASS TEALIGHTS

This delightful project is a great way to use up oddments of lace trim and drinking glasses that have seen better days or have become scuffed in the dishwasher. Straight-sided tumblers work the best because it is easy to wrap the lace around them and sew in place.

Look out for wide lace that will be as tall, or almost as tall, as the glass you want to use. Measure the circumference of the glass and cut a length of lace to fit, with an additional ½ in (1 cm), to allow for a hem at one end. Iron the hem, wrap the lace around the glass, and handstitch in place.

Place a tealight in the glass, light the wick, and be amazed at the pretty glow inside these beautiful lanterns. As with so many things, the effect is so much greater if you group a collection of them together.

inspiration

Patterned jacquard ribbons wrapped around the glasses will give a more exuberant display than sophisticated white lace.

simple WINTER LANTERNS

Old glass jars and odd tumblers make wonderful winter lanterns when wrapped up in the sleeves of woolen sweaters that you no longer wear but can't bear to throw away.

Any small candleholders that fit inside the jar will work, but you can also improvise, using a cut piece of copper piping, for example. If you want to fix the candleholders permanently in the jars, use Superglue or epoxy glue. Otherwise, a very small amount of reusable adhesive, such as Elmer's Tac (Blu Tack) will do the trick.

Making the covers couldn't be easier, and there's no sewing involved! Cut the sleeves off a sweater just below the shoulder, then hold them up to the jars, with the cuff at the top. Cut across the sleeves at the bottom so they are about 1 in (2.5 cm) longer than the jars. Slide them over the top until the cuff is just below the rim, then tuck under any excess sleeve at the bottom.

For the most light to shine through the sleeves, use white candles, but as they won't be visible, it doesn't matter what kind of shape they are in. Tealights work best in short jars and tumblers.

BAKING SET IN A MASON JAR

Mason jars (Kilner jars) are such iconic items, common to so many countries with only minor variations to differentiate the French, say, from the American, the British from the German. The design of them hasn't changed much at all over the years simply because it can't really be improved.

Filling one of these jars with some well-chosen baking tools makes a great gift for any cook, and it makes no odds whether the jar is vintage or new, or has a lever top or a clip closure—the project will work just as well.

Look out for attractive small cake molds and cookie or butter presses, as well as cookie cutters in unusual or seasonal designs, to include in your set. If there's room, add measuring spoons, birthday candles and holders, cupcake wrappers, a pastry wheel, a spatula, and, of course, a wooden spoon. Decorate it with a souvenir spoon or pretty cookie cutter tied with a ribbon, and a tag inspired by our selection on pages 86–9 and 125.

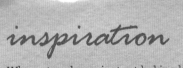

inspiration

Why not make an instant baking kit by including the dry ingredients for cookies or flapjacks in the jar? Include a recipe, then tie with a ribbon and a pretty personalized tag. What better way to get any would-be baker started?

step-by-step SEWING KIT

A sewing kit in a large preserving jar makes a fantastic gift for a friend who likes to sew, for students going off to school or college, or for keeping at your place of work for minor emergencies. You don't have to use the same type of preserving jar as we did—any jar with a screw lid with a pop-out center will do.

☞ **MATERIALS:**

Felt, measuring about 12 in (30 cm) square

Cotton fabric, measuring about 12 in (30 cm) square

Scissors

Glass preserving jar, with a screw top and a metal or glass lid insert

Pencil or tailor's chalk

Pinking shears

Saucer, roughly twice the diameter of the lid, to use as a template

Pins

Small amount of cotton batting (wadding), or similar

Needle and thread

All-purpose glue, white or transparent

Toothpick

Ribbon, about ½ in (1 cm) wide and 12 in (30 cm) long

Sewing machine

Iron

Decorative button

COVERING THE JAR LID

1 Cut the squares of felt and cotton fabric into two. Remove the glass lid from the screw ring. Place the lid in the center of the felt and draw around it. Cut out with pinking shears and put the felt aside.

2 Lay out the cotton fabric and place the saucer upside down on top. Draw around the saucer, then cut out. Place the glass lid, face down, in the center of the cotton circle with the reverse side of the fabric facing up. Fold the fabric around the glass, pinning as you go, to cover the glass. Don't worry if the fabric is slightly loose, as it will need to be to form the pincushion top.

3 Loosen one or two of the pins and carefully stuff in some batting (wadding), making a mound in the center of the lid. Re-pin and stitch all the ends together to tighten the fabric.

4 Spread a very thin layer of glue in the middle of the felt circle and place it over the back of the pincushion, to hide the stitching.

5 Dab a very tiny but even amount of glue around the inside of the jar screw top, just on the top inside edge where the lid makes contact with the glass. A toothpick works really well for this. Press the pincushion into position in the lid and screw onto the jar, not too tightly, and put aside to dry.

MAKING THE NEEDLE CASE

The needle case is really just a tiny fabric book, made like a sandwich with three small rectangles of fabric. We used felt and cotton for the pages of the book, and felt for the cover.

1 Cut out a rectangle, about 3 x 6 in (8 x 15 cm), in felt and in cotton with pinking shears, for the pages of the book. Cut out a second rectangle, slightly bigger all around, for the cover.

2 Sew the ribbon down the middle of the cover lengthwise. Position the ribbon so the extra length hangs evenly off both ends, then machine-sew along both edges of the ribbon for a neat finish.

4

5

☞ **WE ARE SURE YOU WILL FIND MANY THINGS TO KEEP IN YOUR SEWING KIT, BUT HERE IS A GOOD BASIC START LIST**

Needle case

Scissors

Seam ripper

Tailor's chalk

Thimble

Tape measure

Thread spools (cotton reels) in black, white, and gray

Safety pins

Small tin of pins

Odd shirt buttons

Hooks and eyes

5

4 When you fold the book in half, the ribbon will be on the outside. If you just give the book a quick touch of a cool iron, the back spine will flatten. You can then sew one more seam the length of the book, just slightly in from the spine, to complete the book.

3 Lay the piece of cotton fabric right side up on the inside of the cover, then lay the second felt layer on top of that. Pin together, then fold in half and mark the spine of the book with two pins. Sew this line to join all three pieces together, taking care to keep your ribbon ties out of the way!

5 A decorative button is a lovely way to finish off the case. The best place to put it is on the ribbon, just by the cover edge. You can then angle-trim your ribbons and use them to tie the case closed, keeping your needles secure inside.

You may have picked up complimentary sewing kits with useful colored threads at hotels while on your travels, so why not add these to your own kit?

simple WINE IS MINE

Sweet pea rings, designed to attach plant stems to supports, have uses far
beyond the garden. They are perfect paired with a charm for looping around the
stem of a wine glass, to claim the glass as yours. Any charm will do, provided it
has a loop or a helpful hole to thread the wire through. Try game counters, toy
soldiers and animals, cufflinks, old earrings and broken jewelry, or small
keys—whatever takes your fancy.

LABELS AND TAGS FOR HOMEMADE PRESERVES

Making your own jams and jellies, chutney, marmalade, or cordial is a reward in itself. If you have the space to grow fruit and vegetables, it makes sense to bottle and preserve any excess. You may not want to eat zucchini (courgettes) at every meal in early autumn, but making a chutney from them to enjoy in winter is immensely satisfying.

Swapping your own homemade goods with friends and family will expand the range of items you have to try, and the surplus you make in the summer and autumn will come in particularly handy as Thanksgiving or Christmas gifts. A homemade gift is infinitely better than a bought one. What's more, you can personalize it with just the right kind of decoration, which no store would ever do.

Keep collecting preserve jars, soda bottles, and decorative glass containers that come with any kind of secure lid. You may be lucky enough to find a matching set of jars from someone who is having a big tidy-up or downsizing. Let your friends and family know that you want their recycled jars and, provided you give them enough notice, you should never need to buy another container again!

Look out for pages from monthly gardening and home magazines, where the superior paper quality will enhance any label you make. You can overlay part of an attractive image with some colored cartridge or art paper and cut around it with pinking shears or paper edgers, to create a scalloped frame. Hunt down old calligraphy books illustrating different lettering styles to inspire you, and write your message with a fountain pen or calligraphy pen for a real personal touch.

Pages from old books make intriguing backgrounds for labeling—we particularly like vintage cookery books, gardening titles, and home-management periodicals. Keep pages from out-of-date street atlases and pretty gift wrap, to create an attractive border. You might see a lovely image on a cardboard box, possibly a flower with a beautiful shape, that you can cut out to make a gift tag. Use a hole punch and some salvaged string or ribbon to tie it to the jar. Stripy, butcher's-style string is one of the most fitting ways to attach a tag to a food gift. It's simple, looks the part, and comes in lots of colors. We love making "ransom note" labels using letters cut from magazines and newspapers and gluing them to brown luggage tags. The trick here is to collect pages with a variety of lettering sizes, colors, and styles, then cut them out to keep for future projects. As with many simple tasks, we like doing this with an eye on the TV or an ear to the radio. In no time, you will have a stack of letters. Pop them in an envelope and mark the contents so you won't forget. Keep an eye out for attractive numbers as

well, to use on a project like the wall hooks made with ceramic doorknobs (see pages 104–5).

There are so many items that make wonderful and original decorated tags. These are more of our favorites: old photographs; souvenir spoons; salt spoons; tiny butter knives; mini graters; tiny dough (pastry) and cookie cutters; small brown envelopes—pop a surprise recipe inside; lace doilies and fabric circles for covering tops of jars—use pinking shears to give a pretty edging; old buttons; bottle tops with interesting logos—punch holes in them to add as a bottle neck trim (see our lanterns project on pages 132–3); or simply glue them to a luggage tag or the top of a lid.

simple DECORATIVE DECANTERS

For some reason, decanters have acquired a very bad image. As a result, they are often to be found gathering dust in secondhand stores and in the bottom of boxes at flea markets, attracting no interest whatsoever.

If there are small nicks and chips on the stoppers and the rims, absolutely no one wants them, but you should snap them up—they are definitely worth having. Armed with a metal file or sandpaper, try sanding the rough edges until you have taken off the chips and arrive at a smooth finish. The edges may end up a bit wavy and uneven but it is very unlikely that anyone, apart from you, will notice. In addition, you will have gained a real bargain.

Filled with all sorts of liquids, these gorgeous containers, whether they are simple molded glass or fancy lead crystal, take on a new lease of life. Try the traditional approach with liqueurs and spirits, homemade sloe gin, or flavored vodkas. Or infuse olive oil with fresh herbs, such as rosemary and basil, to use in cooking and salad dressings.

For an elegant display in a bathroom or on a dressing table, decant foam baths and body lotions into the bottles and add ribbon trims, with earrings and small brooches attached. Fill old glass mustard pots with a mix of sea salt and lavender flowers for a restorative addition to a bath, or put rosewater or lavender oil in bottles with sprinkler tops. Rosewater makes a soothing skin toner, and the lavender oil can be sprinkled on your pillow to help you sleep.

Of course, these beautiful old decanters can be used for display in their own right, as in our Bottles with Stoppers project (see right). If you are lucky enough to find decanters with their original silver name labels, then try turning them into jewelry (see page 147). One junk-store find could make so many lovely and distinctive things!

simple BOTTLES WITH STOPPERS

Instead of recycling lovely shaped glass bottles that come your way, repurpose them or turn them into decorative items to be admired in their own right.

We used a lever-top bottle that had lost its closure and a recycled cough mixture bottle, with stoppers from pressed glass condiment sets. Old handwritten and torn letters make ornate labels. There are many objects you could hang around the bottle—whatever suits the decoration. This rusty pocket watch complements the label perfectly.

inspiration

Make a brooch with a bottle, attaching it to
the loop of a kilt pin with a jump ring.

Narcisse
'Scarlet

r in

g in any

You

step-by-step MESSAGE IN A BOTTLE NECKLACE

What is it about things under glass like old glass cloches and apothecary jars, that makes them so intriguing? For this miniature message in a bottle, all you need is a tiny clear bottle or vial, a button with a shank, and your chosen "message" that conveys an interest, preserves a memory, or encapsulates a dream.

☞ **MATERIALS:**

Tiny clear bottle or vial, such as a pill bottle or perfume vial

Button with a metal shank

Toothpick

Items to fill the bottle (see below)

Epoxy glue

Old necklace chain or a leather or ribbon strip

Jump ring

1 Fill a clean and dry bottle with your chosen contents. If you are putting any paper inside, very loosely roll the paper around the toothpick and quickly ease it into the bottle, to unfurl. You can use the toothpick to help it along, once it's in place.

2 Mix a small amount of epoxy glue and, with a toothpick, apply it evenly and sparingly to the front of the button, where contact will be made with the bottle rim. Press the button into place and let dry.

3 Once dry, thread the chain through the shank of the button—it makes the perfect hanger. If the chain is too thick to fit, add a jump ring.

`Tiny buttons, seashells, beads, a postage stamp, a small photograph, or a line of words cut from a book or a letter are just some of the many items that could fit inside these tiny bottles and vials.`

step-by-step TEALIGHT GARDEN LANTERNS

It takes quite a few of these lanterns to create any real impact in a garden, so it helps if you can use some very inexpensive and easily found materials to make them. Collect jars, tealight holders, or any small glass container where the rim is wider than the neck, so they can be wrapped around with wire and then hung up.

☞ MATERIALS:

Aluminum garden wire or florist's wire

Wire snips

Glass jars

Old chains, necklaces, or bracelets

Metal tops from champagne corks

Strong hole punch, to pierce metal tops

Jump rings (optional)

Tealight

Thread the cut ends of the wire through the loop you have made. Take the loose ends over the top of the jar to the opposite side and thread them through the wires to make a handle. Secure the wire by wrapping it around itself.

3 To add hanging decorations, loop a chain or other jewelry trim around the neck of the jar, below the wire. If it is too short to go around the entire jar, cut two lengths of wire, wrap around each end of the chain and twist together, to hold the chain in place.

4 Pierce a hole in the edge of each of the metal tops. Thread a short length of wire through each top and tie the ends together around the chain, to make the hanging decoration. Alternatively, attach the metal tops with jump rings. Add a tealight, and your lantern is ready to illuminate your garden.

1 Cut a length of wire at least 5 ft (1.5 m) long—this should be enough for a jar around 2–2½ in (5–7 cm) in diameter. Fold the wire in half and feed the cut ends through the folded end to make a loop.

2 Put the wire loop aound the neck of the jar and tighten so that it is a good fit. Bend the wire back on itself and wrap it around the jar once more.

step-by-step

PATCHWORK MIRROR

Collect or save old mirrors and combine them into one new patchwork mirror. Small, beveled mirrors, square or rectangular, can be combined with cut pieces of a larger old mirror. Find a suitable old frame and custom-make the mirror to fit.

☞ **MATERIALS:**
Old picture frame

Hardboard, cut to inset size of frame

Paper, to make the template

Marker pen

Ruler

Mirror: old beveled-edge small mirrors, mirror pieces, or a large old mirror

Glass cutter

Epoxy glue

Wooden spatula

Small screws and screwdriver

☞ If you haven't cut mirror before, get a glazier to do it for you.

☞ Distressed small mirrors look beautiful and dramatic as a patchwork, set together in an old picture frame.

3

1 Lay the hardboard on the paper and mark the outline. Within that outline, position the beveled-edged mirrors as you wish. Draw around them with a marker pen.

2 Mark out mirror shapes for the remaining space with a ruler. Cut out these shapes from the mirror pieces with the glass cutter.

3 Place all the mirror pieces on your work surface, mirror side down, in the same pattern. Apply epoxy glue to the hardboard and the mirror backs with the spatula. Let the glue set for a minute or two, then re-create your pattern on the board. Use the paper pattern as a visual guide to ensure proper placement. Allow time to dry.

4 Set the hardboard into the frame and secure with small screws. To hang the mirror, attach a wire hanger on the back of the frame or ring hangers on either side.

Chapter
Six

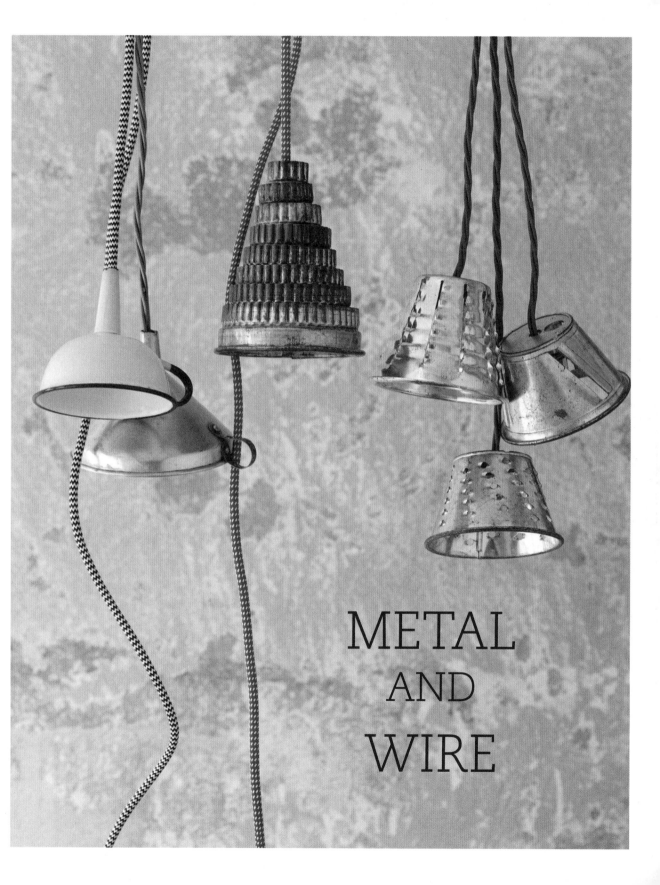

METAL
AND
WIRE

simple
LOAF PAN
WALL SCONCES

Vintage loaf pans, particularly long ones, make beautiful indoor wall sconces. A collection of them, with candles and tealights casting shadows, looks very atmospheric, making them perfect for celebrations, but they can be a permanent fixture, too.

Drill a small hole through each loaf pan (they must be clean and dry) from the inside in the middle, about 3 in (8 cm) in from one end. A clip-on candleholder simply clips on to the bottom edge of the pan, while an eggcup, a tart pan, or a regular candleholder needs to be fixed to the bottom of the sconce with epoxy glue.

To hang the sconce from a wooden wall, simply screw it to the wall through the hole you've made. For a plaster or brick wall, you will need to use a wall anchor (Rawlplug). Use old screws with old pans, new screws with new pans for the best finish.

The best kind of clip-on candleholder has a jointed cuff, which allows the candle to stay upright. Many vintage Christmas tree candleholders were designed this way, to keep the candles vertical on the branches.

simple
FAUCET DRAWER HANDLES

Old outdoor faucet (tap) or valve handles make excellent drawer and cupboard handles, with their open caging, bright colors, and central hole.

You will need screws that are long enough to fit through the central hole and the drawer front, plus an extra 1½ in (4 cm). Put a screw through the front of each handle. Add three or four nuts, to create space between the handle and the drawer. Put the end of the screw through the hole in the drawer. Add a nut and tighten.

simple METAL TIN CUPBOARDS

Old decorative tins with hinged lids make versatile little wall cupboards, particularly for the kitchen, hallway, and bathroom. You can also mount a group of them together for a really effective and good-looking storage system.

Hold the tin against the wall and mark the hanging position. Mark two holes inside the tin, about 2 in (5 cm) below the top, then drill.

Hold the tin against the wall and place a small spirit level on top to check the tin is level—having the lid loose and your hand inside will make this easier to do. Open the lid and mark the two holes through the tin on the wall behind. Take the tin down, drill out the holes, and insert a wall anchor (Rawlplug) into each.

Hold the tin back in place, with the lid open. Put a screw into each hole and tighten into place. If your tin has a small recess on the bottom, which is most often the case, add one or two black rubber washers between the tin and the wall, threaded onto the screw, to achieve a perfect fitting.

Smaller tins, or tins with a portrait format, make an excellent key cupboard. Follow the steps above, but use screw hooks instead of screws. Best of all are screws with an end cap attached or with a separate extra cap. These will cover the holes beautifully and give a great finish.

A tin with a landscape format will give you the greatest storage space. The lid can open from bottom to top or top to bottom, depending on the design, but both will work when mounted on a wall.

step-by-step
GARDEN CHANDELIER

An old wire lampshade can be tranformed into something unique for the garden. Save up broken necklace chains, strands of costume pearls, pieces of silver and crystal to create a garden chandelier. This project is definitely at its best in the evening, hanging in a tree, over an outdoor dining table, or in a conservatory.

☞ MATERIALS:

Fine sandpaper (optional)

Silver spoons and forks

Removable adhesive, such as Elmer's Tac (Blu Tack)

Electric drill

Old metal lampshade from a floor lamp, with a ring in the center

Selection of old necklaces, such as costume pearls, chains, and pendants

Fine wire, such as aluminum garden wire or jewelry wire

Chandelier crystals or glass drops

2 equal lengths of strong chain, suitable for hanging the chandelier

4 small "S" hooks

1 large "S" hook

Glass dish, to fit center fitment

Pillar candle

1 Remove any old fabric or glue from the lampshade. If necessary, rub down with fine sandpaper. Wipe clean.

2 Secure each piece of silverware to a suitable surface with removable adhesive to stop them from moving, then drill a hole through the center of the handles.

3 Hook the forks and spoons onto the chandelier bottom. You may find this easier to do if you place the frame on a lampbase so you can turn the frame as you go and check how the decoration looks.

4 Tie the necklaces to the frame with short lengths of fine wire. Avoid using plastic fishing wire, as this is made to break up and disintegrate quickly.

5 Add chandelier crystals or other glass drops that will catch the light.

6 Attach each end of the heavy chain to the lampshade frame with the small "S" hooks. The chains should cross over each other at a center point and be evenly spaced around the frame.

7 Hold the two chains in one hand and attach the large "S" hook through the links of both chains in the center—the chandelier should suspend evenly from the hook, with the weight taken equally by both chains.

8 Hang the chandelier from a suitable support that can take its weight, which, with the decorations, may be quite heavy. You may need another person to help you with this. Once the chandelier is in place, put the glass dish in the center fitment and the candle inside. Light the candle and admire!

☞ We put our chandelier in a conservatory, where there was no breeze. If you intend to place it outdoors, use a large, wide-mouth glass jar instead of a shallow dish, to stop the candle from being blown out.

☞ As well as crystals, you could also hang small ceramic items, such as tiny pitchers, mini cups, and dolls' teapots, from the chandelier. Give your imagination free rein!

Some silver-plated forks and spoons will be too hard to drill through with a normal electric drill, in which case use jump rings with epoxy glue to hang them (see Salt Spoon Jewelry, page 25).

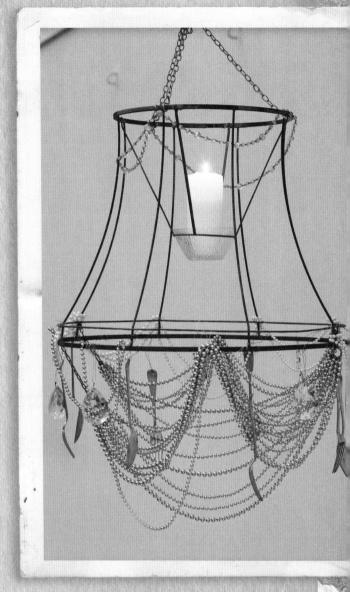

step-by-step
SALAD SHAKER LAMP

There are so many old decorative metal and wire items that can be turned into original lampshades for a pendant light, floor lamp, or table lamp. We used a wire salad shaker, and hung souvenir spoons for decoration from the triangular "drops"—simple components and a project easily completed, with just a little bit of help from an electrician.

4 Lay the spoons face down on the work surface. Dab a tiny amount of epoxy glue on the end of each handle with a toothpick. Add a jump ring, leaving half of the ring hanging off the end of the spoon. Slide a button underneath to keep the ring level with the spoon. Be careful not to get glue on the buttons.

5 When the glue has dried, attach an earring hook (or a second jump ring using needlenose pliers) to the first ring on each spoon. Hang one spoon per triangular "drop," making sure the spoons face outward. Start with one spoon on one side, then add another to the opposite side, and so on. In this way, the shade will remain balanced.

1 Remove the salad shaker handles with pliers. Wash and dry the shaker.

2 Get your electrician to wire up the pendant light fitting to the electrical cord (flex), slot it through the hole in the salad shaker from the inside, and attach it to the wall plug.

3 Hold the pendant light as close to the arm of the floor lamp as possible, and wind the cord around the stand. You can use a small piece of wire to secure the cord to the end of the arm.

Instead of a salad shaker, you could separate one of the wire baskets from the two-tiered baskets designed to store fruit and vegetables. They have a straight edge, rather than the more decorative triangular "drops," but look really effective, too.

Many other unusual and attractive items can be hung from a light like this: chandelier crystals, sugar tongs, vintage clip or drop earrings, in fact more or less anything that you have enough of and which is a similar weight so the light remains balanced.

An electrician could hardwire this light fitting into an existing ceiling light for you. A decorative old ceiling rose would complete the look. There are many interesting ones to be found in metal, ceramic, and porcelain, but you could be more experimental and use a small tart pan to cover a plastic rose!

simple DECANTER LABEL NECKLACE

You don't often see silver, silver-plate, or porcelain decanter labels on bottles of spirits and fortified wines. You're more likely to find them at a flea market waiting for you to turn them into incredibly simple but original necklaces!

You will need to remove the small chain on the decanter label with needlenose pliers. If there are any jump rings, save them to attach the new chain to the label, and keep the small chain for another project (see below).

Use a link chain with a clasp at the back of the neck. Decide where you want the label to sit— on or just below your collarbone looks best—and cut the chain into two equal lengths accordingly. Attach each piece to a jump ring through one of the holes in the label, and there you have it!

This is a great piece of vintage glam for clubbing!

inspiration

If you find more decanter labels, you can link their old chains together with jump rings and make another necklace, adding some silver or faceted beads to the rings for extra bling!

inspiration
PENDANT LAMP

We embellished this salad shaker lampshade with old chandelier crystals in a mixture of styles, one crystal for each triangular "drop." If the crystals don't still have their hooks attached, suspend them with thin wire.

To have your shade hanging, screw a hook in the ceiling above where you want the light. If this is a wooden beam, you can simply screw in the hook. If the ceiling is plaster, drill a hole, insert a wall anchor (Rawlplug), then screw in the hook.

Fix a second hook in the ceiling close to the wall where you want the wire to drop so that it can reach the electric socket. Hang the light, loop the cord (flex) once around the first hook, then the second—this will be enough to hold it in place.

`Clear light bulbs look much better with the wire salad shaker than white or frosted bulbs.`

A nest of pastry cutters creates a fabulous "wedding cake" pendant light; each hangs from the rim of the one before.

step-by-step TART PAN TOWER

Using tart pans in graduated sizes makes an innovative tiered tower, which can be used for all sorts of things, from displaying candles at an outdoor supper to storing vegetables on the kitchen countertop. We pick up tart pans whenever we can, especially vintage ones, which are usually beautifully aged and in excellent condition. As the tower is made of pans in graduated sizes, the individual pieces can be stored nested in each other until you are ready to put them together. That means they travel well, too!

☞ **MATERIALS:**

3 tart pans—small, medium, and large

1 large brioche mold

1 metal breadbasket

4 mini tart pans

Marker pen

Electric drill and drill bit, slightly larger in diameter than the metal rod

Hacksaw

1 metal threaded rod, 3 ft (1 m) long and ½ in (10 mm) in diameter (available from most hardware stores)

5 butterfly nuts

3 large metal washers

2 domed top nuts

Tealights in glass containers and mini tart pans

1 Make sure all the pans, the brioche mold, and the breadbasket are clean and dry. Mark the center of each one and drill a hole.

2 Use the hacksaw to cut the threaded rod so you have one piece about 2 ft (60 cm) long, the other 16 in (40 cm). Put the shorter piece aside to use for the Cake Stand.

3 Start winding a butterfly nut, wings facing up, onto one end of the rod—this will be the bottom of the tower. When you have wound it about 12 in (30 cm) along the rod, stop. From the bottom of the rod, push the largest tart pan, upside down, to the butterfly nut. Then add the brioche mold, the right way up, followed by the breadbasket, rim down.

4 Add a metal washer, followed by another butterfly nut, wings down. Screw the two butterfly nuts toward each other, to tighten up the base layer. Make sure there is some of the rod inside the base, but that it doesn't touch the ground when you stand the base up. Finish the base end of the rod with a domed top nut. Now you can stand your rod up and work from the top down.

5 Screw on the third butterfly nut, wings down, from the top of the rod until it is about 12 in (30 cm)—the distance will depend on the diameter of your pans—from the base layer. Then add a mini tart pan, the right way up, followed by the medium-sized pan, upside down, then another mini tart pan, upside down. Place a metal washer on top, then the fourth butterfly nut, wings up. Screw these two butterfly nuts toward each other to tighten. You may want to adjust the height of this layer slightly now before fully tightening.

Glass and metal containers, such as glass ramekins, mini tart pans, cut-glass bowls, and stemware, will enhance the twinkling effect of the candlelight.

6 Add the final butterfly nut, wings down. This will be your last level so keep things near the top of the rod. If your tower is higher than you'd like, cut off a bit of the top end of the rod with a hacksaw.

7 Add the third mini tart pan, the right way up, followed by the last tart pan, a metal washer, the fourth mini tart pan, upside down, and, finally, a domed top nut. Secure by tightening both nuts.

8 Take a step back and see whether you are happy with the spacing between the tiers—you can always loosen any nuts and adjust the height up or down. Decorate each tart pan with tealights and candles in glass containers and mini tart pans.

inspiration

VEGETABLE TOWER
Vintage tart pans have a wonderful patina, as you can see from this tiered vegetable tower, which is perfect for kitchen storage!

If you make this project with the tart pans facing the right way, you can plant up the pans individually with bulbs, flowers, or succulents, or alternate a planted pan with a pan of candles, and so on. To stabilize the tower, you can use a deeper mold pan at the bottom and fill it with stones or marbles.

inspiration
CAKE STANDS

CANDLESTICK STAND
A single vintage or shiny new tart pan can be fixed to a short candlestick with epoxy glue, to create a beautiful cake stand.

TIERED STAND
A variation of the Tart Pan Tower, with the pans the right way up and a shorter threaded rod.

CANDLE TRAY
Single tart pans make lovely reflective containers for a collection of candles.

simple
METAL TRAY
BULLETIN BOARDS

Old decorative metal trays make excellent bulletin boards—look for the steel ones that are magnetic, not the aluminum ones that aren't. Trays are always to be found at flea markets and are generally very inexpensive.

We decided to fix our kitchen bulletin boards permanently to the wall. Drill two evenly spaced holes in the the middle of a tray, checking that they line up with a spirit level, then drill corresponding holes in the wall for wall anchors (Rawlplugs). Push screws through the holes and screw them into the wall anchors. The screws should be only slightly smaller than the holes so that the tray won't move once in position on the wall. Any notices and magnets (see right for some delightful ideas for making your own) will cover up the screw heads.

A simpler, temporary way of hanging your tray is with an expanding picture hanger. As a bulletin board like this generally carries little weight, a picture hook or even a nail will be sufficient. You could also thread some cord through holes in the tray, knotting the ends in front and have a hanging loop at the back.

inspiration
VINTAGE
MAGNETS

Round magnets are easy to come by in hardware stores and craft stores. They are inexpensive and it is great fun to customize them.

Apply Superglue or epoxy glue to the non-magnetic side of a magnet and attach the vintage decoration of your choice. It couldn't be simpler. Suggestions for decoration include: old coins, medals, metal toys, game counters, buttons, jewelry, wooden jigsaw puzzle pieces, wooden and plastic dice, watch faces and other broken watch parts, bottle tops, badges, and souvenir charms.

LAMPSHADE COFFEE TABLE

Wire lampshade frames are one of those wonderfully versatile junk finds. Always inexpensive, they come in a huge range of sizes and styles, and lend themselves to so many interesting uses, such as this simple coffee table.

You can use the lampshade, which must be in good condition, right side up or upside down—it usually depends on how large you want the tabletop and how stable the frame is. Once you've decided, look out for old round glass or mirror tops that are about 4 in (10 cm) larger in diameter than your lampshade, to give a good overhang, but the size really depends on what you can find and the diameter of your shade. If you decide to buy a new top, glass stores will often have them in stock.

Strip the shade of all its fabric and lining, then wash it with soap and water. Once it is completely dry, use epoxy glue sparingly around the top edge of your lampshade, to secure the glass in place.

A large old lampshade frame can also be turned into a table base for use in the garden or on a patio or balcony, as well into a bedside table.

TOFFEE HAMMER LIGHT PULL

This is such a simple project and one that gets noticed. Instead of a toffee hammer, you could use any similar weighted item that has a means of threading through the ribbon.

☞ **MATERIALS:**

Tape measure

Ribbon

Sharp scissors

Iron-on interfacing, medium to firm weight

Tailor's chalk

Iron

Sewing machine

Toffee hammer

Needle and thread

1 Measure a piece of ribbon to the length required for the hammer to be at a convenient height to pull. Double the length, then cut the ribbon.

2 Cut a length of iron-on interfacing that is around 8 in (20 cm) shorter than the ribbon—you don't need interfacing for the ends of the ribbon tied around the toffee hammer—and a little narrower in width so that it it will sit hidden inside the fused edge of the ribbon. Mark the ribbon 4 in (10 cm) from each end with tailor's chalk and then place the interfacing on the ribbon starting at the chalk line. Iron in place.

3 Fold the ribbon in half widthwise and pin together. Machine-stitch the length of each side of the ribbon from the chalk line, securing the interfacing inside. Leave the ends open.

4 Cut the cord of the original light pull as close to the ceiling as you can but allowing enough length for threading it through the folded ribbon and tying in place. Tuck the end of the cord inside the ribbon so it doesn't show.

5 Thread the ends of the ribbon through the hole in the hammer, crossing them over each other, and tie together in a knot. If you feel that the ribbon might undo itself, make a few handstitches through the knot to secure it. Cut the ends with pinking shears.

step-by-step PAIL HOSEPIPE TIDY

Galvanized steel or enamel pails (buckets) drilled into an outside wall, and close to an outside faucet (tap), make novel as well as practical hosepipe tidies.

☞ **MATERIALS:**
Galvanized steel or enamel pail (bucket)

Pencil

Electric drill

2 large heavy-duty wall anchors (Rawlplugs) and screws, suitable for an outside wall

2 rubber washers, to fit screws

Screwdriver

1 Mark two holes in the bottom of the pail, one in the middle, the second above the first, halfway between the middle and the rim. The handle hooks should be at the sides, to allow the handle to hang down out of the way when the pail is screwed in. If the pail is decorated, ensure the decoration will be on top like ours.

2 Drill out both holes to a size that the screws will fit in tightly, to make a more secure mount.

3 Hold the pail in place against the wall. Mark the position of the pail holes on the wall. Drill the holes. Insert the wall anchors (Rawlplugs).

4 Hold the pail back against the wall, with a rubber washer at one hole, to make the fitting more secure. Screw the pail into place. Repeat for the second hole. Wrap the hosepipe around the pail.

Use the pail to store a bar of soap and a nailbrush, and the handle to hang a towel—just the thing for cleaning up after toiling in the garden.

A hanging birdcage looks gorgeous at night filled with candles. For the garden, you could plant a birdcage with a vine.

simple
BIRDCAGE LAMP

I am not sure why we love old birdcages so much but we do, and our favorite way of using one is to wire it up and make a light. Some cages easily convert to pendant lights, but this small version with feet is perfect as a table lamp. Placing ornaments inside, such as vintage ceramic birds is a lovely touch. Or you could go mad and decorate it with little figurines, as we did!

Clean your birdcage thoroughly with dishwashing liquid. When completely dry, drill a hole through the bottom in the center.

Ask an electrician to wire up the cage using a light fitting, electrical cord (flex), and cord grip, for the underside of the cage. Light fittings are available in ceramic, plastic, or metal. Choose one that will allow you to use a fairly small light bulb, preferably a filament bulb, which will look more attractive.

Once the light is in place, you can use the cage door to access the switch. Alternatively, have the electrician use a non-switch light fitting and fix a switch to the cord.

Chapter Seven

FURNITURE
AND
FURNISHINGS

step-by-step
DROP-IN SEAT COVER

These drop-in seat chairs are very easy to come by, and the seat covers can be made in less than 30 minutes with just a few simple tools, transforming the most unpromising junk-store find into something quite special and individual.

1 Lay the dishtowel right side up over the seat and move the towel around so you can decide where the pattern will fall best. Mark the towel accordingly with tailor's chalk.

2 Cut around the dishtowel, adding on a sufficient amount (a minimum of 1½ in/4 cm all around) for tucking and securing under the seat. If you wish to pad out the seat, cut the batting (wadding) to the correct size first, then make sure you allow enough fabric to go over the batting as well. Always measure twice to be sure before you cut.

3 Place the cut dishtowel back over the top of the seat, right side up, and wrap it around and under the seat. (If you are using wadding, place it over the seat first, then put the dishtowel on top.) Use masking tape to hold it in position under the seat.

4 Start to secure with pushpins, small tacks, or staples, as you prefer, pleating the dishtowel into the corners, so that it sits neatly over the seat. Stretch the towel as you go until it is attached all the way around and is flat and crease-free on the seat. Insert the seat into the chair.

inspiration

Old oil paintings on canvas also make stylish seat covers. Follow the instructions above but avoid stretching the painting as you would the dishtowel—this will crack its surface. Pay particular attention at the seat corners, pleating the painting carefully to give a smooth finish.

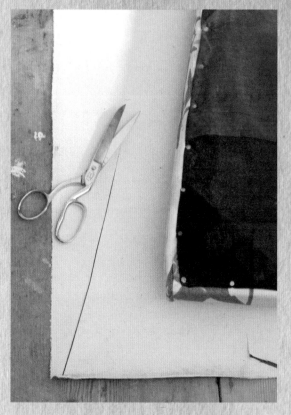

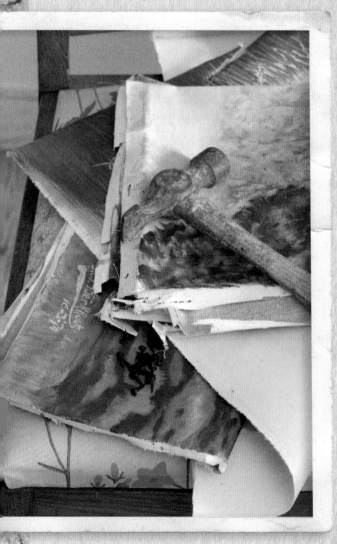

You can use any piece of fabric that appeals for this project, as long as it is fairly hardwearing and will cover the seat with a good margin on all sides. However, if the fabric you choose is thick, wrap it around the chair seat first before cutting to make sure it will fit in the frame.

step-by-step REVAMPED SOFA CUSHION COVERS

The original chesterfield sofa used for this project is a perfect example of a piece of furniture that has become rather down-at-heel over time but its solid construction means that it still has plenty of life left in it. All it needs to restore it to its former glory is a revamp with new seat cushion covers.

☞ MATERIALS:

Tape measure

Sharp scissors

Tweed fabrics for the patchwork and cushion band

Sewing machine with zipper/cording foot attachment

Needlecord or wool fabric for the underneath of the cushion and the zipper band

Zipper

Iron

Pins

Cord

Strips of fabric for the cording (piping)

Tailor's chalk

Yardstick

1 Measure the seat cushion, including the length and width of the band around the seat, and the length of the zipper band section. The zipper band needs to be long enough to go around one side (generally the back) of the cushion and to wrap around the two back corners—this will make it easier to insert the cushion in the cover. The zipper itself should be at least 3 in (8 cm) shorter than the band.

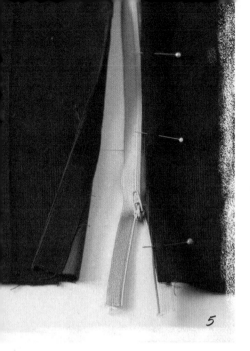

5

2 Choose your fabric combination for the patchwork, then cut out individual patches to make up one larger piece that will form the top of the cushion so that the finished patchwork is at least 2 in (5 cm) bigger all around than the top of the actual seat cushion. Remember to include 1 in (2.5 cm) seam allowances around each patchwork piece. Machine-stitch the patches together.

3 Cut out the fabric for the underneath of the seat cushion, adding a 1 in (2.5 cm) seam allowance all around. Any fabric of a suitable thickness, such as a plain wool or needlecord, will do because it will not show on the finished cushion.

4 Take the measurement for the zipper band, then add on a 1 in (2.5 cm) seam allowance all around and a further 2 in (5 cm) for insetting the zipper. Cut out the needlecord or wool fabric to size, then cut this down the middle to make the two pieces either side of the zipper. Take the measurement for the rest of the cushion band, then add on a seam allowance as above, so that the cushion band will match the zipper band in width when the zipper band is made up with the zipper inserted. Cut out the tweed to size, but do not cut in half.

7

5 Turn in a 1 in (2.5 cm) seam on one long side of both zipper band pieces and press. Machine-stitch a short 2 in (5 cm) seam at one end to secure the zipper at the closed end. The other end will be left open. Place the zipper behind the pressed edges, pin, and stitch along both sides. Use a zipper foot for a professional finish. Pin the zipper band to the cushion band piece at each end to form a circular band.

6 To make the cording (piping) for the top and bottom of the cushion, cut two lengths of cord, each one to fit the perimeter of the cushion. Then cut out your chosen cording fabric on the bias, allowing

8

This is one of the more time-consuming and involved projects in the book. It would be best to allow a couple of days to complete it.

sufficient fabric to encase the cord, as well as a 1 in (2.5 cm) seam, which will be inset into the cushion.

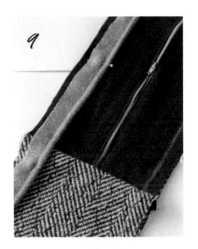

7 To join the bias strips, place two fabric ends together at right angles and machine-stitch at an angle across the two pieces. Repeat until you have one long strip of fabric with joins at an angle. Fold the fabric in half lengthwise. Repeat the above for the second length of cording.

8 Insert the cord into the folded fabric strip and machine-stitch using the zipper/cording foot, which will give you a much tighter finish.

9 To place the cording on the cushion band, mark the required seam lines on the band by drawing two lines with tailor's chalk and a yardstick on the right side of the fabric—these will form the top and bottom stitching lines. Pin the cording to the lines with the stitching line of the cording following the chalk line. The corded edge faces inward, with the raw edges facing outward. Machine-stitch both pieces of cording in place.

10 Mark the four mid-points of the edges of the cushion band with a pin—these are important for matching the band to the patchwork and the underneath of the cover. Mark the same four mid-points on the edges of the patchwork top and the underneath of the cover. Measure and mark the seam lines all around the two pieces by drawing a stitching line with tailor's chalk.

11 To assemble the cover, match the cushion band to the four pins on the patchwork. Pin together. Then start to pin outward from the four pins toward the four corners. When you reach the corners, clip the fabric of the cording to allow it to expand and curve into the corners, giving the required right-angle curve. Make at least four or five small cuts within the seam allowance to create this curve.

12 Machine-stitch the band in place and then repeat the same task for the underneath of the cushion cover, leaving the zipper partly open so you can turn the fabric inside out. Once you are happy with the fit, stitch again around the two top and bottom seams to reinforce them. Clip the edges to neaten. Turn the cushion cover the right way.

If, as with our sofa, your cushions have become a little saggy and worn out, you can either stuff the original seats with cushion pads to fill out the gaps or treat yourself to a new set of cushion inners.

step-by-step
MEDICINE CABINET

This lovely vintage cupboard is the perfect size for a bathroom cabinet and for hiding away the medicinal paraphernalia that we all seem to hoard. The detailing on the door and the glass-fronted panel give the piece real character, as do the pages from a 1930s medical booklet used to line the inside. The medicine adverts are quaintly old-fashioned, entirely appropriate for the cabinet.

☞ MATERIALS:

Old cabinet or small cupboard with glass door

Screwdriver

Sandpaper

Damp cloth

Masking tape

Black paint suitable for wood surfaces, enough for three coats

Paintbrush

Wallpaper or pages from a book

Wallpaper paste

Metal polish

Fabric for the curtain panel, such as an old towel or dishtowel

Tape measure

Pair of metal knitting needles, for curtain rods

Pen

4 small screw eyes

Spirit level

Scissors

Needle and thread

Wall anchors (Rawlplugs) and screws

1 Remove any catches and latches with a screwdriver. Rub down the surface of the cabinet and the shelves with sandpaper until you have a smooth finish for the new paint. Wipe down the surfaces with a damp cloth to remove any dust and allow to dry completely. Stick masking tape around the inside and outside of the glass, to protect it from the new paint.

2 Apply enough coats of paint to give a dense, solid color. We painted the outside, the inside of the door, and the shelves but decided to leave the inside of the cabinet to add to the vintage charm.

There is no need
for an undercoat
if you are
painting over
an existing
painted surface.

3 Once the paint is dry, use wallpaper paste to stick the wallpaper or book pages to the back of the cabinet—keep repositioning the pages until you get the look you are after. Replace the catches once the wallpaper is dry. If the catches are made of metal, clean them with metal polish first.

4 To make the curtains, measure the the height and width of the glass, allowing an extra 2 in (5 cm) above and below the pane so that the fixing cannot be seen from the outside. Cut the fabric accordingly.

5 With a pen, mark at the top and bottom of the door the positions of the four screw eyes that will hold the knitting needles in place. Check that they will not impede the opening and closing of the door. Screw in the eyes, using a spirit level to make sure they line up.

6 Cut the curtain fabric to size using the position of the screw eyes as a guide and allowing extra fabric top and bottom for making a casing to hold the knitting needles. To make sure that the panel fits exactly, stitch the casing on the top side only and double-check the exact turning required on the bottom edge by hanging the curtain inside the door. Once you are happy with the fit, stitch the bottom casing.

7 Slip the knitting needles through the screw eyes on the opening side of the door and thread the curtain onto the needles. The second inner set of screw eyes will hold the curtain in place. Fix the cabinet to the wall with wall anchors (Rawlplugs) and screws.

`To give the shelves a distressed vintage look, sand them lightly with fine sandpaper.`

inspiration
BUILT-IN MIRRORED CABINET

This is such a great idea for almost any room in the house that has a cavity wall with plasterboard. You can use a framed mirror, even a framed painting, to create a practical and good-looking cabinet that is flush with the wall—incredibly useful and space-saving! The project does take a bit of planning but it's well worth keeping it in mind if you are undertaking any home improvements.

hinges and a magnetic closure, and attach the mirror to the cabinet frame. Depending on what you plan to store in the cabinet, you can add small shelves inside. In a tiled bathroom, you can tile the back of the cabinet, to give a really smart finish.

The mirror needs to be small enough to fill the gap between any two upright wood supports in a stud wall. The width is more important than the height, which is more flexible. Box out the void in the wall in wood to the same dimensions as the mirror. Add

step-by-step
MAP TOP CARD TABLE

Card tables are handy items of furniture because they fold flat and can easily be stored away. They are ideal for outdoor summer parties or for entertaining a few extra guests in the house. However, the traditional felt top isn't always suitable, so changing it for a new cover gives the table a more varied and practical use.

☞ **MATERIALS:**
Card table

Screwdriver

Craft knife

Newspaper

Old sheet or blanket

Fine sandpaper

Colored wood varnish, to match existing wood

Paintbrush

Dustpan and brush

Tape measure

Map, at least 1 in (2.5 cm) larger all round than the card table

Pencil

Scissors

Wallpaper paste and paintbrush

Soft, clean cloth

Clear matt artist's varnish

1 Unscrew the wooden surround on the top of the table to remove the old felt. The felt should come away easily, but if not, use a craft knife to cut it.

2 Place the card table on newspaper with a blanket or sheet underneath to catch the dust and any varnish spills. Rub down the areas of wood that will be visible with fine sandpaper.

3 Brush off any dust, then wash the wood with soapy water. Let dry. Following the manufacturer's instructions, paint on the varnish in thin, even strokes for a smooth coverage. Let dry. If required, apply a second coat.

4 Measure the top of the table and mark the dimensions on your map with a pencil. Cut around the map outside your pencil marks by an extra 1 in (2.5 cm) all around so that the edges of the map can be secured underneath the wooden surround.

5 Apply wallpaper paste to the top of the table with a paintbrush. Press the map down onto the paste, easing away any excess by smoothing the top of the map with a soft, clean cloth. Let dry.

6 Paint a thin, even layer of artist's varnish over the map to seal it. Let dry.

7 Replace the wooden surround by screwing the screws back into place.

Your new card table will have a wipeable surface but will not be suitable for hot items. Use a heatproof mat when serving hot food.

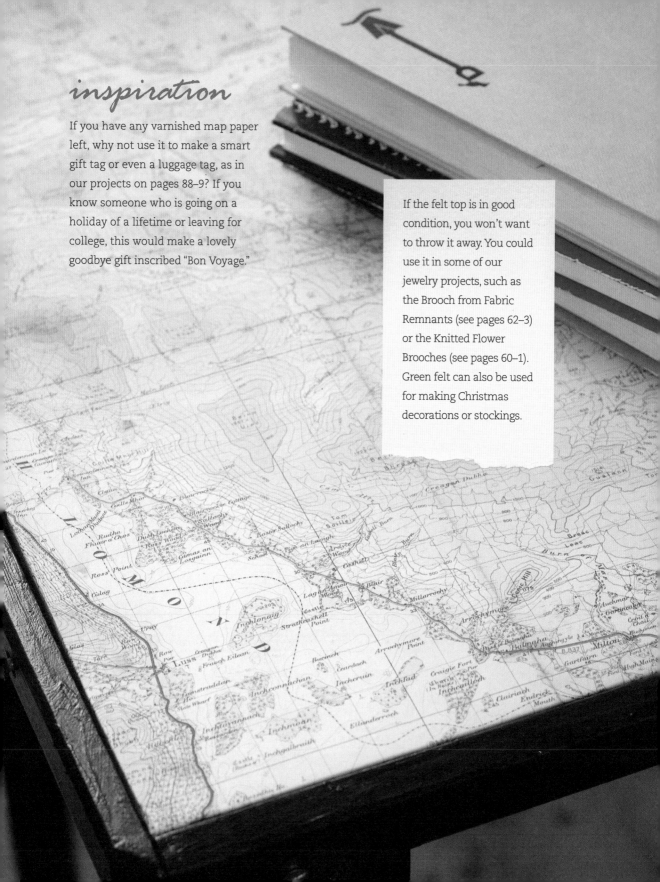

inspiration

If you have any varnished map paper left, why not use it to make a smart gift tag or even a luggage tag, as in our projects on pages 88–9? If you know someone who is going on a holiday of a lifetime or leaving for college, this would make a lovely goodbye gift inscribed "Bon Voyage."

If the felt top is in good condition, you won't want to throw it away. You could use it in some of our jewelry projects, such as the Brooch from Fabric Remnants (see pages 62–3) or the Knitted Flower Brooches (see pages 60–1). Green felt can also be used for making Christmas decorations or stockings.

Instead of using varnish, you can seal the map with plastic laminate film. Measure the dimensions as for the map, then cut to size. Starting at one side, place the film over the map, peeling off the backing as you go to stick the film without any creases.

NECKTIE CHAIR SEAT

step-by-step

The seat of a small chair or stool, drop-in or wrap-around, can be given a new lease of life reupholstered in neckties. Friends and family will doubtless donate ties, or you can buy them for next to nothing at thrift stores (charity shops).

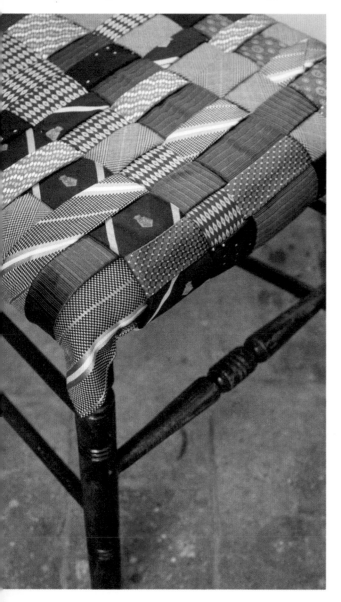

☞ **MATERIALS:**
12–18 men's neckties, depending on the size of the seat

Iron

Small chair or stool

Pins

Small tacks and hammer or staple gun

Scissors

Needle and thread

White glue

1 For a wrap-around seat cover, select two neckties for the front corners of the chair. Unpick the back of the ties down their spine and press flat, leaving the lining and interfacing in place. Lay one tie diagonally across the seat, with the wide part of the tie at the front, so there is enough to hang down and cover the corner. Pin in place. Pull the tie firmly to the opposite corner, but don't overstretch it, then pin in place at the back. Secure the tie at the front with a tack or staple on the front edge of the chair, on either side of the leg. Secure the tie at the back with a staple underneath the frame. Repeat the process with the second tie for the other corner. Don't worry if the tacks or staples at the front show—they will be covered as you progress.

1

2

Be as conservative or as creative as you like with your choice of neckties: use all silk ones or mix the fabrics, restrict the colors, or make a rainbow, go for solid patterns or combine stripes with dots.

2 Lay out more neckties on the seat, leaving 3–4 in (8–10 cm) of each tie hanging over the front, sufficient to wrap under the chair later. Make sure the ties cover the seat, without any gaps between them but don't let them overlap. For a perfect fit, you might have to reverse a couple of the ties, to prevent any gaps. Alternating tie designs work best, to create a good repeating pattern on the seat.

`If your chair seat is wider at the front than at the back, it may look better to have all the wide end of the ties at the front, so they fan out following the shape of the seat.`

3 Once you are happy with their position, pin the ties in place, then secure with tacks or staple to the underside of the front of the chair. Do the same at the back of the chair.

4 Starting at the front of the chair, weave the narrow ends of the remaining ties across the seat through the secured ties in an under-over basket-weave pattern. Wiggle the ties into place as close as you can to the previous tie but without overlapping. Secure the ties with a pin at each side, leaving enough excess tie at each end to wrap under the seat. Secure with tacks or staples.

4

5 Add the tie to cover the front edge of the seat last. Secure with a few handstitches.

6 Glue any cut ends of the ties into place under the seat to prevent them from fraying.

3

inspiration

For a drop-in seat, you will need enough length to wrap around the seat to secure on the underside, so don't cut your ties until you have worked out the "front to back" length for a square seat, or the "side to side" length for a rectangular one. From here on, follow steps 2–6, as above.

There's no need
to strip off any
existing fabric
or vinyl on the
seat—the neckties
will cover it
completely.

step-by-step
DÉCOUPAGE CHEST OF DRAWERS

Rather than paint an item of old "brown" furniture white, we took a painted chest of drawers back to its original state and gave it a vintage, textured look. The découpage flowers and cake molds make very pretty decorative details.

☞ **MATERIALS:**
Old painted chest of drawers

Old sheet or blanket

Newspaper

Screwdriver

Paint stripper and large paintbrush

Old cloths

Sandpaper

Wire wool or scouring pads (optional)

Electric drill

Small vintage cake or cookie molds

Drawer handles with new longer screws

Scissors

Illustrations from an old book

White glue

Clear matt artist's varnish and small paintbrush

1 Stand the chest of drawers on an old sheet and newspaper outdoors. Unscrew the drawer handles. Put the drawers to one side.

2 Following the manufacturer's instructions, apply paint stripper to the rest of the chest that will be on show. Allow the paint stripper to penetrate the layers of paint—you will find that it tends to take off one layer at a time. Apply as many coats as you need for the desired distressed look.

3 Clean the surface with old cloths. Dispose of any removed paint and newspaper in the garbage. If the chest is at all sticky, wash it with soapy water.

4 Rub down the surface with sandpaper: use coarse sandpaper if you want to remove more paint, or fine sandpaper if you have already achieved the effect you want. Instead of fine sandpaper, you could use scouring pads or wire wool. Wash the paintwork thoroughly and let dry.

5 Sand the drawer fronts with medium to coarse sandpaper to allow the paint and wood to show through. Once you are happy with the look, brush off any dust and wash them with soapy water.

6 Drill a hole in the center of one of the molds that will allow the screw of the new handle to fit through. Place the mold upside down in position on the drawer front and place the handle on top, lining up the holes. Push the new screw through the hole in the drawer from the back and screw it into the back of the handle. Repeat for the other handles.

7 Cut out the illustrations for the découpage and stick onto the drawer front with white glue. Seal with artist's varnish.

This project is easily adapted to make a narrow desk using an old scaffolding board (see page 183).

simple
WALL-MOUNTED DRESSING TABLE

Using old wall brackets is a great way to make a very cool dressing table. Narrow and off the floor, this dressing table is the perfect solution for a small space.

Choose your brackets—wooden, cast-iron, or galvanized metal—according to the style you want for the room.

Use a spirit level to work out the position of the first bracket and mark with a pencil. Drill holes where appropriate for your bracket. Insert wall anchors (Rawlplugs) into the wall, then screw in the screws.

Work out the position of the second bracket. Rest a yardstick across both brackets, place the spirit level on top in the middle, and adjust the position of the second bracket, if necessary. Mount the second bracket to the wall, as above.

Add a shelf on top. With deep brackets, there is no need to secure the shelf further.

inspiration
CRATE TABLE

Sturdy old wooden crates make excellent small pieces of furniture. Use them singly to make a bedside table or in multiples, vertically or horizontally, to create a larger piece.

Where you position the crate on the wall makes all the difference to how smart it looks. We sat ours on a pair of metal L-brackets above the baseboard (skirting). Using wall anchors (Rawlplugs) to secure the brackets and crate in position provides good support, and the fixings are all but invisible.

Resources

This list is deliberately eclectic because it is made up of all the special places we have discovered for ourselves, whether for work or for fun. We have included some of our favorite car boot sales and flea markets, too. All of them are great locations for finding wonderful junk.

UK

Paper & Stationery Suppliers

Cavallini & Co.
www.cavallini.com
Distributed in the UK by: The Paperie,
1 Grey Friars, Chester CH1 2NW
01244 342691
www.thepaperie.co.uk
Decorative papers

Cornelisen and Son
105 Great Russell Street, London WC1B 3RY
020 7636 1045
www.cornelisen.com
Papers, pens, gilding materials, inks

Paperchase
213–15 Tottenham Court Road, London W1T 7PS (and branches)
020 7467 6200
www.paperchase.co.uk
Papers, general artists' materials

Rossi of Italy
www.rossi1931.it
Decorative papers, stationery; contact website for UK stockists

www.thepapermillshop.co.uk
Lovely papers online from James Cropper's paper mill in Kendal, Cumbria

Independent Hardware Stores

Cummins Hardwares
62 South Street, Dorking, Surrey RH4 2HD
01306 882559
All the materials and advice you could need

Dockerills
3A Church Street, Brighton BN1 1UJ
01273 607434
www.dockerills.co.uk
Great family-run, old-style hardware store

Heathfield Ironmongers
108 High Street, Heathfield, East Sussex TN21 8JD
01435 862626
Ironmongery, housewares; superb service

Household Supply Stores
54 Devonshire Road, Bexhill, East Sussex TN49 1AX
01424 210779
Lots of essential ironmongery bits

Craft & Fabric Stores

Calico Kate
36 High Street, Lampeter, Ceredigion SA48 7BB
01570 422866
Huge emphasis on patchwork fabrics

Greenbridge Works
Fallbarn Road, Rossendale BB4 9AG
01706 260649
Great place for discount furnishing fabrics

Greens Fabrics
Ciceley Lane, Blackburn, Lancashire BB1 1HQ
01254 680954
Excellent bargain dress fabrics

Hobbycraft Stores nationwide
www.hobbycraft.co.uk

John Lewis Stores nationwide
www.johnlewis.com

Penbanc Fabrics
Crymych, Plas y Ffynnon, Newport, Pembrokeshire SA41 3XB
01239 820568
Absolute treasure-trove of fabrics

The Quilt Room
37/39 High Street, Dorking, Surrey RH4 1AR
01306 740739
www.quiltroom.co.uk
Beautiful selection of printed fabrics; haberdashery

Stephen Walters
Sudbury Silk Mills, Cornard Road, Sudbury, Suffolk CO10 2XB
01787 372266
www.stephenwalters.co.uk
Very old weaving mill with outlet store

The Stitchery
The Riverside, Cliffe High Street, Lewes, East Sussex BN7 2RE
01273 473577
Plenty of sewing and knitting staples as well as some great printed dress fabrics

Truro Fabrics
Lemon Quay, Truro, Cornwall TR1 2LW
01872 222130
www.trurofabrics.com
Two massive floors of haberdashery, fabrics, yarn; very helpful service

Vanners Silk Weavers
Gregory Mills, Weavers Lane, Sudbury, Suffolk CO10 1BB
01787 372396
www.vanners.com
Amazing bargains from the factory store

Vintage Bird
48 High Street, Hastings, East Sussex TN34 3EN
01424 433300
www.vintage-bird.com
Superb selection of furnishing fabrics

Wayward Remnants
68 Norman Road, St Leonards, East Sussex TN38 0EJ
0781 501 3337
Amazing vintage haberdashery; textiles

Car Boot Sales
Check details with fellow carbooters.

Brighton Marina and Racecourse.
Marina: Sundays, year-round;
Racecourse: Sundays and Wednesdays, year-round
Carmarthen Showground. Sundays from 7am, year-round
Carew Market and Car Boot, Tenby. Sundays from 7am, year-round
Dorking, Surrey, station carpark, Sundays from 6.30am, year-round
Fontwell Race Course, Littlehampton, West Sussex. Most Sundays, April to September
Icklesham, near Rye, East Sussex on the A259. Sunday mornings, April to October
Nash Street and Rainbow Farm, Upper Dicker, Hailsham, East Sussex on the A22. Sunday mornings, April to October
Polegate, Eastbourne on the A22. Sundays, April to October

Fairs, Markets, & Events

International Antiques & Collectors Fairs
Organizes big antiques fairs outside London,
including Ardingly, Newark, and Builth Wells
www.iacf.co.uk

Leicester Indoor Market
Humberstone Gate LE1 1WA
www.leicestermarket.co.uk
Bargain fabrics and haberdashery

Longsight Market
Dickenson Road, Longsight, Manchester
M13 0WG
Fantastic fabric bargains

Victoria and Albert Museum
Cromwell Road, London SW7 2RL
020 7942 2000
www.vam.ac.uk
Check for ethical fashion swishing events;
links to creating your own swishing party

Antiques/Secondhand Stores

Lewes Antiques Centre
20 Cliffe High Street, Lewes BN7 2AH
01273 476148

Snoopers Paradise
7–8 Kensington Gardens, Brighton
BN1 4AL
01273 602558

Architectural Salvage

www.salvo.co.uk
Online site for finding salvage throughout
the UK; information on fairs and events

PARIS

Street Markets

Port de Vanves
Avenue de la Porte de Vanves 75014
Our absolute favorite. Saturday and Sunday
mornings until lunchtime

Fabric & Craft Stores

BHV Rivoli
55 rue de la Verrerie 75004
Haberdashery as well as paints, papers—
almost a whole floor—and a basement of
hardware and tools

Entrée des Fournisseurs
8 rue des Francs Bourgeois 75003
Ribbons, wools, and a fantastic selection
of buttons

Marché Saint Pierre
2 rue Charles Nodier 75018
Floors of different fabrics

Mercerie Moline
2–6 rue Livingstone 75018
Haberdashery

Rougier et Plé
13–15 boulevard des Filles du Calvaire
75003
Good general craft store with an excellent
selection of paper

UltraMod
2–3 rue de Choiseul 75002
Wonderful museum piece of a store with
original fittings, stuffed with treasures

Bead & Jewelry-Making Stores

La Compagnie des Perles
50 rue des Archives 75004

Matière Première
12 rue de Sévigné 75004

NETHERLANDS

www.ijhallen.nl
Huge monthly indoor and outdoor flea
market

www.jandegrotekleinvakman.nl
Traditional haberdashery store

www.mijnpakkiean.nl
Gorgeous well-edited haberdashery and
old patterns

www.verzamelaarsjaarbeurs.nl
Vintage Collectors' Fair, twice a year over
a weekend; fantastic for European goods

www.vliegerpapier.nl
One of the world's best paper stores

www.wallpaperfordelight.nl
Fantastic resource for vintage wallpaper

SWEDEN

NUD Collection
Fristad Industri AB Lightcity, S 513 33
Fristad, Sweden
www.nudcollection.com
Fantastic lighting and colored cords

USA

Antiques/Junk Fairs

www.127sale.com
www.alamedapointantiquesfaire.com
www.antiquescapital.com
www.junkbonanza.blogspot.com
www.renningers.com

www.brimfieldshow.com
One of the best, in Massachusetts

www.roundtoptexasantiques.com
Texas antiques fair, great atmosphere!

www.whiteelephantsale.org
Very curated antiques/junk fair, with all
proceeds going to the Oakland Museum,
CA—an amazing annual event

Architectural Salvage

www.salvo.us
Online site for finding salvage throughout
the US; information on fairs and events

Lighting Sources

Architecturals
PO Box 9978 Philadelphia, PA 19118 0978
800 658 5096
www.architecturals.net

Grand Brass Lamp Parts
51 Railroad Avenue, West Haven, CT
06516
www.grandbrass.com

Van Dykes Restorers
PO Box 52, Louisiana, MO 63353
800 558 1234
www.vandykes.com

Index

Sending our thanks...

We would both like to thank Holly Jolliffe, our brilliant photographer who coped with every kind of weather and lighting issue the winter threw at us! Also, Cindy, Sally, Dawn, and Clare at CICO; Laura, our designer; and Helen, our lovely 'grace under pressure' editor! Also, thanks to Chris and Andy at the antiques emporium Eras of Style in Bexhill on Sea, and to Rhod and Jim at the hidden gem that is the walled garden at Ashburnham Place, near Battle.

From Juliette: Special thanks to Paula Jones for the professional piping tuition masterclass; Barbara Fredriksson and Louise Roberts for their resources tips; and, of course, Robin for all those meals, furniture stripping in the cold, and endless cups of tea!

From Stacy: Special thanks to Lucy Malcolm, for making our doll personae, with all the attention to detail (see page 7)—they look just like us! And a big thank you to Adrian Egan, builder extraordinaire, for sorting out last-minute panics with a smile.